# Woody Tales, Tall but True.

## Living; Working and Playing in New Zealand's wild places.

Enrico Hoover

Publisher, Enrico Hoover.

ISBN 978-0-473-73830-3

# Contents.



Throughout this book, the 'Bogor' cartoons are the work of Burton Silver. (See page 9)

**About the Author.**

Enrico (Harry) Hoover started at the Golden Downs Woodsman School as a 16 year old, fresh from school, in January 1971, finishing his training at Totara Flat at the end of 1973. He was posted to the Waipoua Kauri Sanctuary (Northland) in 1974 and after spending some time working with the exotic logging gangs in the forest, he left the Forest Service for the thrill of driving Log Skidders for a private logging contractor.

A visit home to his parents for his 21st birthday saw him offered a job in Twizel driving big machinery, and very soon, some of the workshop guys taught him enough about welding to enable him to sit and pass a Welders ticket, which led to being offered work with the Ministry of Works and Development as a welder, helping to make the penstocks which would eventually carry the water from the canals to the powerhouses. Fabricating / Engineering of one sort or another occupied his life from then on, interspersed with 18 years as a Territorial Soldier (grunt, driver, medic), as well as obtaining a Driving Instructors licence and spending time as an Engineering / Welding tutor and Driver Training. At age 47, a desire and a passion for excellence in shooting sports led to him doing degree studies for a Bachelor of Sport and Exercise Sciences degree, including a Coaching degree, which led to some excellent personal performances in both pistol and rifle shooting sports, as well as developing an interest in balance and proprioceptive training with the Wobbleboards that he has now been making and selling for over 20 years.

Serious ill health has meant plenty of surgery, and, with his wife Hilary, who has also had her share of medical issues, after 35 years in the Waikato they emigrated south to build their forever retirement home on the banks of the Mataura River at Fortrose in the Catlins. That is still a work in progress, as finance and health issues allow.

Having been a writer of sports related / coaching magazine articles for many years, at the 2023 Woodsman Reunion in Nelson he volunteered / was arm twisted to put together a book of tales about life as a trainee Woodsman. This book is the result.

**Co Authors.**

Many Woodsmen and other forestry people have all contributed to this work. Often, the stories came to me from more than one person; They were often just tales told around the table and occasionally, I have no clear recollection of who actually told me what. So if you recognise a tale that's yours but I haven't mentioned you, my apologies and my thanks. You'll also see several stories told by many people, with a slightly different slant, so for the sake of the story, I've left those items in.

The contributors to these tales are many, some are anonymous, and some don't want their names used or known. The photos also came from many of us, often the same photo came from more than one person, so obviously we shared.

I would like to acknowledge with thanks the contributions of; Campbell Barrowman, Reid Mallinson, Lindsay Arthur, Mike Bange, Peter Christie, Greg Heaven, Colin McKinney, Terry Johnstone, Sally Quickfall, Chris Bennett, John Currie, John Stent and especially Dennis Wastney for the great collection of books he gave me. These guys and gals have actually co-authored this book.

**Preface**

It is with pleasure that I have the opportunity to contribute to this book of recollections of a number of my former colleagues, those who commenced their careers in the Woodsmen Training Scheme.

My first posting as a Technical Trainee, as we were called, was to King's Camp down the road from Golden Downs village and the Woodsmen's Hostel. I was aware, as everyone was, of Woodsmen and their reputation so I must admit to a perhaps traditional view of their place in the organisation. Countering this, I would have to say that as time went by I developed a respect for the behaviour of the characters I met and certainly for their attitude to what was pretty hard work. This is something that has always stayed with me and was the start of the increasing regard I had for Woodsmen and for their training scheme.

There are a number of reasons for the success of the Woodsmen Schools, one of these being to the credit of the Department and the other to those who completed their training and took their place in the Forest Service or elsewhere.

I believe that our Department set up an excellent programme and organisation to lead raw young appointees from a home and school life through to becoming part of a respected community. This required imparting the skills and attitude necessary to get on with life, a daunting job, but achieved under the guidance of competent field staff and others charged with personal development of the individuals. I'm sure that any readers will know what I mean.

Another factor, perhaps unexpected initially, was recognition of the fact that you can't keep good people down. Original thoughts that Woodsmen would tend to be restricted to skilled labouring positions overlooked the fact that many of the appointees possessed skills that could lead to supervisory and managerial roles, and this proved to be the case.

Enough lecturing from me, now is the time to read and enjoy recollections of the ‘good old days’. I hope that doing so will give you well deserved pride in your achievements.

Peter Herrick
formerly
Conservator of Forests.

## Woody Tales.

It was a different world, a different place and time, and a hard way of growing up. For those of us who made it through, the New Zealand Forest Service Woodsman Training Schools gave

fabulous and excellent opportunities for learning a wide range of skills. Personal growth and development, hard work, excellent skills, fun and laughter, friendships and bonds that would last a lifetime.

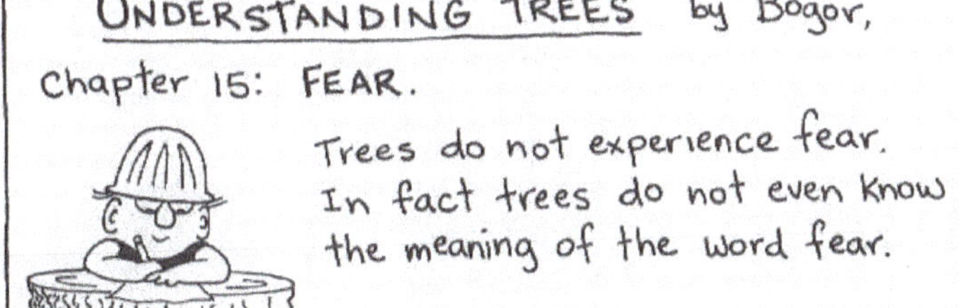

*Note.* This book is not intended to be a history, it's more of a collection of memories by and about people, many of whom are no longer with us. Some of the events described were hurtful to those who had even a small part to play in whatever happened. For that reason, wherever possible, I have used just the Woodsman nicknames of the characters, although many of us didn't like our nicknames. Or maybe just a name and an initial. The Woodies involved know who you are or were.

Some of the things we got up to would land us in jail today, many would cause us to lose our jobs. Actually, it's a wonder that we survived to adulthood. Some didn't.

*How much Wood could a Woodchuck chop if a Woodchuck could chop Wood?*

## Acknowledgement.

Throughout these pages there are some photos from Woody days and Forestry days. I've attempted to focus on what we did, not who or what we were. Also included are some excellent cartoons about a Woodsman named Bogor. His creator, Burton Silver, is a superbly talented New Zealander who has given me permission to use his 'Woodsman' cartoons. Thank you very much Burton. At the time, everyone I knew within the Forest Service loved Bogor, and most still do. These clips are here to provide a chuckle, although if you can find a deeper meaning, "fill ya boots".

## Introduction.

The New Zealand Forest Service Woodsman Training School system took young men, mostly fresh from school, or perhaps with a year or two of work under their belts, to join a community dedicated to learning the 'Skilled Crafts' of Forestry, and to provide a workforce to manage New Zealand's timber industry. There were three main schools, Kaingaroa in the central North Island, Golden Downs, near Nelson at the top of the South Island and the Dusky School at Tapanui in Southland. Other smaller schools were at Berwick, Aupouri, Ashley and Totora Flat.

These training schools were places where young men (mostly only teenage boys really), were taught how to handle the tools of the trade; mattocks, saws, axes, chainsaws. Also, big machinery; trucks, bulldozers, log skidders, log loaders. Firefighting equipment; pumps and hoses. Firearms and all forms of hunting and trapping were a big part of the culture. And as you might expect, booze. We could be a rowdy lot.

This book is a collection of stories about the lives of a few of the people who went through the system. Some spent their entire working careers within Forestry, some went on to other careers, some to the armed services, both Regular Force and Territorial. Many of our instructors came to forestry from the armed services, from war or conflict zones, and once home, they needed civilian careers. Along the way, there have been a lot of funny stories, some sad, some downright terrible, some that today would have us labelled as sexual deviants or worse.

All the stories are what made us who we are today.

In general; Strong capable people who have a love of life and each other, a love of hard work and even harder play. We certainly weren't angels, but, as tough as it might have been at times, most of us wouldn't change a thing.

My personal experiences are from Golden Downs, my understanding is that the other schools were also very similar environments, similar conditions and learning experiences, so unless otherwise mentioned, life at any of the schools all followed the same patterns.

Mostly, these stories are from and about the Woodsmen, but one gal went through the same ordeals as us Woodies, she worked just as hard, if not harder, and she loved her forestry life every bit as much as the guys did. So her story is here as well. She has well and truly earned her place in this book.

## A Brief History.

The Golden Downs Woodsman School was started in 1951 and continued until 1982, with other Woodsman schools in both the North and South Islands; Kaingaroa (1952-1981), Dusky / Berwick (1965-1981), Aupouri (1974-1981), Ashley (1978-1982). I'm told that Totara Flat was also an official school but I haven't been able to verify this yet. Suffice to say that many Woodies went to Totara Flat for their 3rd year, and from there worked in Granville Forest and then up and down the entire West Coast.

At that time (40's and 50's), there was a very real need to train a cadre of workers to manage the growing need for exotic forests and timber production in NZ.

There are already many excellent books, videos, DVD's and YouTube clips dealing with the forest industry in NZ, the history, the politics, the reasons for and the hopes thereof, and none of that is in the scope of this book.

The first Europeans to visit NZ recognised the potential value of our timber trees, as the UK was already running out of suitable timber to construct naval vessels, not to mention all the other uses English oak was put to. From the history of logging in early European New Zealand (the first recorded tree felled by Europeans was in 1772), to the Saw-milling industry, to the Forest Service itself, there has been an ever growing demand for New Zealand's timber, and it's value to the country.

For much of the 20th century, labour to manage the forests was beset with a multitude of problems, ranging from a shortage of workers to hazardous work conditions, housing, wages, and much more besides. Prior to the Woodsman schools there had already been Timber Cruising schools, Hunter schools and Timber Grading schools, so it seems to be a logical progression to establish the Woodsman and Ranger Schools.

## The Lifestyle and the Work.

During my first year (at Golden Downs), we lived in one of 2 hostels with about 40 rooms (20 either side), of a main corridor, with a recreation room at one end, a manager's flat at the other end and an ablution block set off to one side. For our second year we were moved out to individual huts located alongside the hostels, and for our third year we were able to apply to a forest elsewhere in NZ to participate in other forms of forestry craft that may not have been available at Golden Downs, Dusky or Kaingaroa schools. Personally, I have never been to Kaingaroa or Dusky.

We had a cookhouse where we all ate, and from memory some of those meals were appalling. Over the years, many different systems were tried; cooks on contract, cooks on wages, catering staff drawn from the ranks of the trainee Woodsmen, wives or family of other Forestry staff. None worked particularly well. The packed lunches we were issued daily were a joke at the best of times, disgusting at the worst.

My main memory is of a cook we called 'Bull Moose' who was a very thin, scrawny old man, always grubby, always with a fag in his mouth, usually with an inch of ash hanging off it, often falling into the porridge as he ladled it out to us. At breakfast every day we were given a packed lunch in a brown paper bag, which usually consisted of several sandwiches with marmite and lettuce, or 'horsecock' (what looked like thinly sliced dogfood roll), and lettuce. If we were lucky, we got a bit of cheese or perhaps a few baked beans on margarined bread. We occasionally got a piece of fruit as well. My memory aside, I don't think any of us starved to death and I certainly didn't loose weight on what we ate. I remember most of us were hungry all the time. Most of us have never touched 'horsecock' again in our lives.

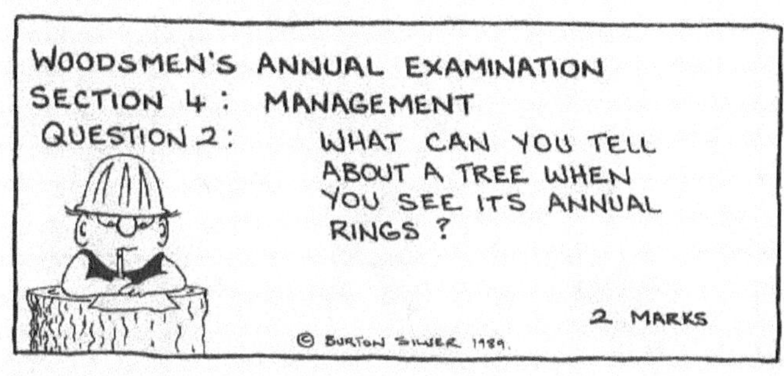

For anyone reading these stories who wasn't a Woodsman, the basis of our training was (initially anyway), actually just as cheap labour for the government.

Some of the basic skills we were taught were;

**Planting.**

This involved the use of mattocks or spades to plant pine trees in perfectly straight lines across many miles of hills. Each planter followed a visual reference, a 'pole line' which consisted of Manuka poles, standing upright in a line across the hills creating a visual reference system which allowed each planter to follow an exact line and easily check whether he was on or off his correct line. At any given spot, the planter could look ahead and if he was on his correct line he would see one pole on the horizon. If he was off course, he would see two poles. Using this system made it easy to stay an exact distance away from the guys working either side. Earlier Woodsmen had other systems, ropes and other ways of maintaining exact distances which gradually evolved into the pole line method.

Being in the 'Poling gang' was a welcome break from planting. The poling team had to be well in advance of the planting gang, and once a pole line had been used, ie., the trees had been planted, the poles were recovered and then set out on a new piece of country. It wasn't unusual to have thirty of forty guys, side by side (six feet apart), working their way across a hillside, planting trees as fast as they could. A steady supply of trees needed to be kept up to the planters, sometimes there were dedicated tree carriers, sometimes we walked back and resupplied ourselves. During the day, everyone occasionally needed a bathroom stop, so generally one would go back down your line of trees till you were out of sight, and 'fertilise' one of the trees you'd recently planted. Occasionally someone would fertilise ahead of where the planters were, and obviously you deposited your offering on someone else's line. This created quite a bit of hilarity, words such as "You F-ing Mongrel" would echo up and down the valley as someone discovered the atrocity that had been perpetrated upon them.

Much of the Golden Downs Conservancy is gravel country, officially the Moutere Gravels. This of course meant that we were often planting in a gravel base as opposed to nice soil, and to ensure seedling survival, some dirt is required. As you'll see from some of the stories, this meant occasionally carrying and planting dirt as well as the seedlings. As well as Woodsmen gangs carrying out planting operations, there were also contracting gangs, and it seemed to many Woodsman intakes (at the time), that the contractors were given the blocks where they could achieve higher planting rates (therefore higher earnings), whereas the Woodsmen (on trainee wages), were given the more difficult blocks where higher planting rates weren't possible.

***Note. Different species of trees required different spacing between the seedlings and this data was supplied by the scientist type people from the FRI (Forest Research Institute).***

## Release cutting.

This involves using slashers to cut away undergrowth from around the pine trees which had been planted a few years previously. Depending on where we were, the undergrowth could be any growing thing, but generally gorse or bracken fern, blackberry or toot*. Sometimes up to 3 or 4 feet high (1 meter +). Prior to planting trees, the land was usually burned to create an ideal growing medium for the new trees and so not only did the new pine tree seedlings do well, but so also every other species of plant, which of course would then compete with the young pine trees and would generally smother the pines within a year or two. Release cutting after several years of seedling growth gave the pines a better opportunity to stretch out of the undergrowth. Of course, once the tree emerges from the undergrowth it provides a canopy under which the undergrowth cannot live well and so the tree is able to aim for the sun while the undergrowth dies off.

**Note. Toot (TUTU) is a very easily identified Native plant (Coriaria) which contains a neurotoxin, poisonous to animals and humans. It can also cause bees to produce toxic honey, causing occasional illnesses but the last fatality was in the 1890's.*

## Pruning.

For pine trees to produce the best possible timber (knot free), it is necessary to remove the branches from the trunk of the tree, and this is done in stages. When the tree is about 6 to 10 years old the branches are removed from the ground up, using saws, secateurs or loppers of some sort. The branch is cut from the trunk (as closely as possible), the wound then heals creating a 'green' knot in the wood which doesn't reduce the strength of the eventual timber.

Over the years the branches are pruned in stages, for example, Low Pruning (0-6 feet), Medium Pruning (6-10 feet), High Pruning (10-20 feet), Ultra High Pruning (20 feet and up). These numbers vary with the species of tree, and different tools are used for the different heights of the pruning. High pruning may involve the use of a pole mounted saw, ultra high pruning involves ladders or can involve climbing of the tree itself. There were trees which were pruned to the height of the ladder, then the Woodsman stood on a branch, pulled the ladder up the trunk and tied it to the tree, then continued climbing and pruning till the desired height was reached, then back down to ladders end, relocate the ladder back to ground level, prune of the last remaining whorl of limbs and climb down the ladder. Some tree species can be self pruning and may just need some encouragement to shed their branches.

Not every tree is pruned. When they were planted, the seedlings were spaced apart a certain distance to optimise competition and growth. Then in years to come, the density of the trees needs to be reduced to encourage further growth, and so the trainee Woodsman must learn to evaluate the trees with the best potential to be a great timber tree, and only prune those stems which will be eventually kept as future trees.

**Axe Thinning.**

Initially, to encourage trees to grow as fast and as competitively as possible, the trees are planted at very close spacings. 6 feet between trees, and 6 feet between lines was used for Pinus Radiata, other species such as Douglas Fir had different requirements. This gives a certain number of 'stems per acre', or, once we metricated, 2 metres x 2 metres giving X number of stems per hectare. As the trees grow they spread and by the time they are 10 years old they are getting too big for the available nutrients in the ground and so their growth rate begins to slow. To maintain the growth rate, the trees are now thinned. This is a perfect opportunity to teach Woodsmen trainees how to fell trees, without the huge danger of cutting down full size trees. Give a 16-year-old Woodsman an axe, a file to sharpen that axe, and let him loose on a hillside where 2 out of every 3 trees must be chopped down. These lads are still not big enough or strong enough (or mature enough), to handle chainsaws, and besides, there are some skills to be learned first.

Sometimes the trees are big enough to be cut down and used for making fence posts (post thinning), sometimes (and possibly terrain dependant), the trees are cut down and left to rot on the ground (thinning to waste). Imagine a hillside covered in trees about 30 - 40 feet high. The trees were planted in lines, so each Woodsman takes a line and starts to work their way along the line, evaluating the best trees to leave and the best to remove. Usually, the best trees have already been selected during the pruning processes. Trees with poor growth, deformities such as double headers, or simply mis-shapen are removed.

Using their newly sharpened axe, the tree is scarved, then back cut, to fall in the intended direction. The sound of "Timber" being shouted every time a tree falls echoes across the hills as 30 or 40 or 50 Woodsmen work their way across the hills.

Because the trees are growing quite densely at this point, it's not uncommon for a falling tree to get caught in a neighbouring tree and therefore, to get 'hung-up'. Having a hang-up means more work, as one must then chop the hung-up tree into smaller lengths to get it to fall completely to the ground. It can't be left as a hang-up as that's dangerous, it could fall at any later time and kill or injure someone. Generally, these trees are small enough for the feller to be able to push it somewhat, or to encourage it to fall in the correct direction. If physical strength doesn't get the hang-up down and, chopping the tree into post size lengths doesn't seem appropriate, there is always the 'fun' option. Taking one's axe in hand, and because this is probably a tree that still has all its branches (i.e. it hasn't been pruned), it's generally quite easy to climb to the top of this felled but still standing tree. Generally this tree will now be leaning at an angle (often about 60 - 70 degrees), making it easier to climb. Once the upwardly mobile Woodsman gets near the top of the tree, he uses his axe to chop away the branch or branches that are holding the tree up in the canopy, and as the tree begins to fall, the Woodsman throws his axe clear and then just holds on to a couple of branches and rides the falling tree down. As the tree hits the ground the underside branches provide enough cushioning to allow the tree to bounce a bit, reducing the impact of the fall to safe levels, at least as far as the Woodsman is concerned. It's great fun,

it helps develop a cool set of skills as well as making the day's work a bit more adventurous.

I'm pretty sure that nowadays, OSH (Occupational Safety and Health), might take a dim view of this sort of practice. After a few months of this work, we had built a bit of muscle, learned a few skills and were ready to learn……..

**Chainsaw Thinning.**

Depending on when a Woodsman started at the Woodsman school determined what sort of chainsaws he would first learn to use. In my case the saws were 'Canadiens'. I don't recall the specs, but they were heavy, loud and had no anti-vibration systems.

In years to come, a lot of people including myself, developed Carpal Tunnel injuries and diseases such as 'White-finger', which was the damage or destruction of the nerves in the hands due to the heavy vibration of these tools. At the time that I was in my second year at the Woodsman School, the most popular saws in use in the professional logging gangs were Dolmar, Stihl and Husqvarna, but these saws were for professionals, us Woodies got cheap stuff to learn on. McCullock, Echo and Canadien are the brands that I remember.

Obviously, chainsaw thinning went a lot quicker than using an axe. The tool still needed regular sharpening, more often if you hit a stone or dug the bar nose into the dirt. Our axes hadn't liked stones and dirt much either. With an axe one just carried a file. With a chainsaw one needed petrol, bar oil, brush for cleaning filler caps prior to refuelling, chain files, spanners and other tools for bar and chain maintenance. Chainsaws require considerable care and attention, mistakes are costly and permanent, as well as potentially very messy. At least when you slice a toe off with an axe it's a nice neat cut.

**Logging.**

The Forestry industry is of course, geared to the production of timber with which we make homes & furniture, bridges and road signs, paper for writing on and paper for wiping stuff off with. Pencils are made from wood, as were everything from clothes pegs to roof and wall shingles. The art of felling a tree and then turning it into usable products has many thousands of books and an endless supply of internet clips devoted to the subject. From the Woodsman's point of view, we were taught to fell trees using time honoured methods such as axe and saw before we were considered old enough and wise enough to learn about chain saws.

Obviously, a chain saw is not a tool for the fainthearted; as with any dangerous tool it requires a high degree of knowledge and ability. In my time as a Woodsman, we didn't yet have chaps (safety trousers which would stop a spinning chain), but helmets and earmuffs were in use. Chainsaws didn't yet have safety brakes or anti vibration handles, we learned to use the tool with common sense and physical dexterity.

**Timber Cruising.**

This craft was learned by many Woodsman trainees, and before the Woodsman Schools existed, there were specialist Timber Cruising Schools, specifically run for people to learn the skills of gathering information about the timber that existed in our native forests. To be a 'Timber Cruiser', one had to love being in an outdoor environment, sometimes seven days a week. If you were going to work in some of New Zealand's remotest places you needed to be able to get there on foot and carry everything you were likely to need, not only to do the job but also to survive well while you were doing it. Essential items were a backpack, a Swandri jacket and a large brimmed hat. We generally wore short pants as they don't stay wet all day, even if one is working in snow or rain.

The general idea is that you measure and catalogue every tree of millable size in a given block of land, as well as collecting information about terrain, topography, etc. The information is used by the land owner or government department to determine such things as the millable value of timber on a certain piece of land, whether the timber is accessible, what species are available, the potential for putting in roads, etc.

## Native Forests.

Huts and tracks within our forest parks used to come under the auspices of the NZ Forest Service. Trainee Woodsmen were sent out to learn the practical, 'hands on' skills of building wire rope swing bridges, huts, shelters, tracks, and any and all other paraphernalia that goes with such outdoor places. Drilling holes in rock, using explosives, setting anchors and bolts are all part of the job, with plenty of spade and shovel work, as well as doubling as pack horses. If you need to make concrete in the bush, we didn't always have the luxury of carrying it in by chopper or packhorse. And of course, hunting and trapping and poisoning the wild animals that frequent those places was also a part of the lifestyle. Needless to say, if we didn't learn to cook well using a campfire or camp oven, we didn't eat well. Living and working in the wild places was a dream job for many of us.

## Timber Grading.

The Forest Service provided staff to monitor the activities at privately owned logging companies and sawmills around New Zealand. Obviously, the amount of sawn timber that emerged from the sawmill needed to tally with the amount taken from the hillside, discrepancies could result in major disputes, altercations, even from time to time, fisticuffs. Methods of payment changed over the years; when the payment was based on the amount of timber produced by a mill it meant that the cutting of the log into usable timber could be a bit lax. When the saw-miller had to pay by the volume of the log he had bought, it meant that the mill had to be operating at best efficiency. Not everyone liked the changes in policy, so it was important that the Woodsman Timber Grader got it right.

## Burnoffs.

Once a block of land has been clear felled, i.e., all the standing timber has been removed, it needs to be brought back into full production of growing trees as soon as possible. The best way to prepare land for the growing of trees is to burn off the waste / slash from the logging process. Fire is of course a natural process. In nature, lightning starts fires which clear the

undergrowth and provide an ideal, nutrient rich environment for seeds to germinate. In managed forests, there are usually blocks of land covered in growing trees alongside the recently logged area, and of course the forest operator doesn't want those trees harmed. So, we learned how to burn off blocks of land in the middle of existing forests. There is not only a very

precise science to managing fire but it's also hot, hard, and potentially dangerous work. Existing forests are protected from the burnoff block by physical firebreaks as well as good use of weather. Wind and weather conditions, as well as good management, is critical. As Woodsmen, we were tasked with the physical aspects of any burnoff, not the science and / or the management of those aspects. We lit fires with various methods, we carried pumps and hoses when necessary. We set them up and used them according to the wishes of Management. We drove fire engines, we managed hot spots and accidental sparks getting away into standing timber. Some of the tools, such as flamethrowers, were particularly fun to operate, but potentially very dangerous work. Working one's way on foot through dense scrub with a flame wand to the bottom of a gully, lighting a fire and then getting out of the way of the spreading flames was occasionally a hair-raising skill.

## Boarding School Mentality.

The hostels we lived in were ideal places for the senior boys to indoctrinate, bully and harass the new chums, and this often became excessive. If there was any actual thinking behind this it was the old doctrine of 'it'll make a man out of ya'. Many of our instructors were men who had been Woodsmen trainees and graduates from the schools themselves, and many of them also actively encouraged the boarding school mentality to continue. Often various hazing / harassing / bullying activities were done by just a couple of guys with sometimes many others watching on. I heard about one guy (nicknamed Sergeant), who was bullied, hit and repeatedly dragged though a deep puddle by a couple of Woodies who were then and also later in life, seen as the elite. Sergeant left that day, never to return. I've often wondered, what would he and others have achieved in life if he hadn't been forced to quit. There was a 'sort of' enquiry that night from Management, wanting to know who had been involved, and several people who watched but didn't participate put their hands up. But the guys who did the beating didn't. I guess our ethics change during our lives, and we all do things that we come to regret.

## Research.

Research was always ongoing to find better ways of growing timber faster, and often Woodsmen were involved in various trials of one sort or another. Not all these experiments had the Woodsmen's best interests at heart.

Experiments were conducted to find more efficient ways of thinning blocks of trees, for a time, poisoning seemed like a sensible option. During the late 1960s, Woodsmen worked in the stands of trees that needed to be thinned, one worker making his way along the tree line cutting a notch in each tree to be removed, followed by another Woodsman carrying a modified knapsack pump filled with various poison solutions. There were many poisons used or tested, various concoctions which used the most harmful chemicals, and of course, the Woodsmen wore the standard issue safety gear; shorts and singlets, or t-shirts. In colder weather, perhaps a bush shirt or Swanni. The knapsack pumps leaked, or if you bent forward a bit they spilled from the lip. They were of course designed to carry water to hot spots at a fire, not chemicals. It wasn't long before many of the guys started developing rashes and sores, but Management weren't inclined to take the complaints of junior labourers seriously.

Eventually a group of guys put down their sprayers and refused to use the poison. They would still cut the notches in the trees with axes, but they wouldn't use the sprays. Foremen ordered them to continue work, they refused and were then made to walk back to headquarters from the top of Reay's Saddle (7-8 k's). On arrival at HQ they were told, "If you refuse to work, you're all sacked". Several of the group stood their ground and said that they would contact the State Services Commission or the Public Service Association. Several phone calls later, the group were told by someone in PSA to "sit tight, don't work, we'll be there shortly". The next day a representative flew down from Wellington and the proverbial 'shit hit the fan'.

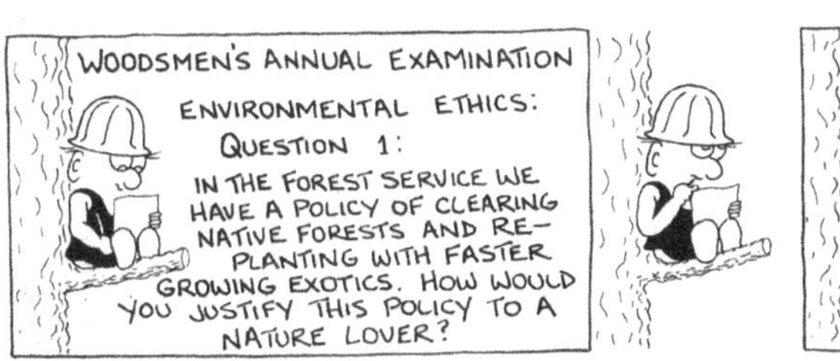

At one forest (Balmoral), a poison thinning operation went badly wrong. Every tree in the block died, not just the ones which we poisoned. Investigations didn't reveal the cause until a fire engine load of water was blasted into the root system of a few trees and it was discovered that the tree roots had grown into each other so effectively that the entire block was one single tree root system with many thousands of spars sticking out of the ground. It was eventually discovered that because of the underlying gravel the tree roots had just spread out into the surrounding dirt and the trees hadn't put down the main tap root that pine trees are well known for.

New and better systems were devised, one system saw a Woodsman carrying a small, motorised unit on his back, a hole was drilled into a tree and the hole was then injected with an arsenic compound which came from a storage container on the backpack. The arsenic was considered safe for human contact. What wasn't realised at that time was that arsenic poisoning is accumulative and so the Woodsmen, still in their basic shorts and singlet safety gear were getting daily exposure. This eventuated in multiple illnesses and possibly, the underlying cause of 'who knows what'?

As late as the early 1970's Woodsmen were still using chemicals such as 245-T, or 24-D with no protective clothing, and for a while in 1972 there were a group of Woodsmen at Golden Downs who, within a few days of starting work with these chemicals, were experiencing unusual symptoms; fingernails and hair growing so rapidly that fingernails needed cutting weekly, hair more often. I was told by the Matron that the way 24-D or 245-T killed plants was to cause the cells to grow so rapidly that they burst, and of course, that's the stuff we were using. (Agent Orange, the defoliant used in Vietnam was these same chemicals). Perhaps it had a similar effect on humans? It would be interesting to find out how many of us suffered the same effects that our servicemen in Vietnam did? Did we develop cancers in our later years because of being exposed to these poisons? I suspect we'll never know, and who would have the balls to open this can of worms?

Another research project was the high-altitude planting of multiple species of trees at various altitudes in order to ascertain what species did best at what altitudes?

In the winter of 1972, a group of about 12 Woodsmen with a Foreman, were sent to the Beeby's Range to plant trial plots of about 20 different species of pine trees. Pinus Pallustris, Pinus Pinaster, Pinus Contorta, Pinus Nothofagus, Pinus Radiata, Pinus Elliottii, plus an assortment of Firs. These are some of the species I remember, no doubt there were many others.

We lived in a hut near the top of the mountain, and daily, we laid out sample plots and then planted our seedlings. For example, 100 x P. Radiata seedlings would be planted at a certain altitude, then 100 meters above that a plot of a different species, then another 100 meters up, another species, all the way up the hill. The intended outcome was that there would be a stand of each species in the trial at every altitude on the mountain. We were often working well above the snow line, the conditions were harsh and the accommodation and supplies rudimentary.

We had a small articulated tractor (a Holder), for moving the tree supplies around the hills, and the Kea with whom we were sharing the hillside took great delight in ripping the Holder's tyre treads apart. One of the lads threw a rock at a Kea to knock it off the tractor, and with the Kea lying on the ground winded, and us being told to get on with our work, someone had the bright idea of keeping the bird and making a pet of it. But how to keep it while we went about our day's work? An empty 10 litre kerosene tin was handy, so we quickly cut the bottom from the tin and upended it over the bird with enough rocks to hold it down. When we arrived back at the hut that night the tin was still there, with the rocks still holding it in place, but the side of the tin had been ripped open from top to bottom and the bird in the hand was now a bird in the bush, so to speak. An amazing bird, smarter and stronger than any of us.

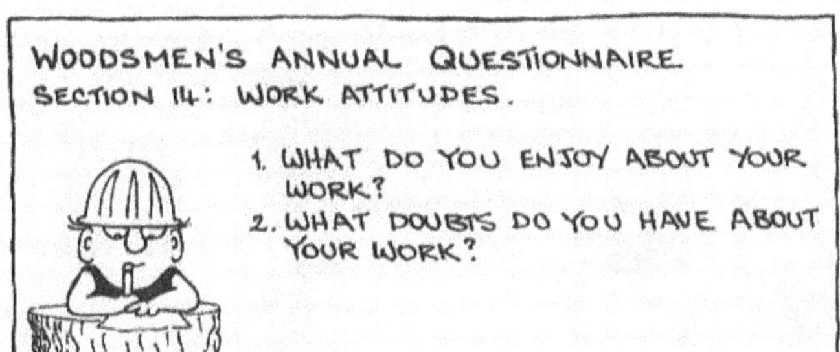

Our high-altitude trial planting came to a halt with the first big snowstorm of the season and we were trapped in the hut. For a week or so it was just an adventure, a bit boring perhaps, we just lay around the hut stoking the fire and drinking cups of tea. Then we ran out of food. When we could get the radio to work, all we could hear was that the weather was too bad, and we couldn't be rescued. Eventually, the decision was made to walk out, so that is what we did. Downhill carrying out all our gear, down frozen hills, and waterfalls, but with none of the gear needed for such a trip. We made it successfully but I'm sure that was more due to luck than good management.

## Nicknames.

One of the many interesting things about the Woodsman Schools was the nicknames that we all had. Most of us accepted them, some of us hated them. This book of tales will mainly use only our nicknames, we all know who we are or were. Some of the tales are about people who are no longer with us, some are about people who would be too embarrassed to have their identities made public and most of us have long grown out of our nicknames, except perhaps amongst ourselves. Snorkel, Rat, Faggot, Flange, Goober, Dino, Bojangles, Reverend, Duh, Bluey, Squeak, Spider, Butch, Lux, Yakimo, Jawbone, are just some from around my own years.

Some are obvious. Snorkel was very tall and somewhat thin, Fats is self-explanatory, Squeak was very small and mouse like, both in size and disposition. CatRooter was a guy who loved searching for old bottles and any antique memorabilia / scrap he could find, so his forays into gorse bushes, blackberry and other prickly stuff often left his legs scratched and bleeding, as if he'd been trying to root a cat (this is the polite version).

Any reason at all was good enough for a nickname, and once you had it, it was yours whether you liked it or not.

Many years before I joined the Forestry, one Christchurch lad (Brent T) was initially nicknamed Daffodil, because his then girlfriend was called Rosemary (No, it doesn't really make sense). But then he had to be renamed Dick Turpin, because Dick rode a horse called Black Bess, and Brent's new girlfriend was a rather dark, large bottomed lass. No, there is no rhyme or reason to it, other than the twisted logic of a group of youngsters finding a laugh in everything. Years later I worked in Waipoua Forest (Kauri Sanctuary) with Dick Turpin, he was a good workmate and we had lots in common. Dick actually left the Woodsman school after his first Easter there; he couldn't handle the bullying. He went home to Christchurch where he brooded for the long weekend, and then changed his mind. He came back to Nelson and successfully finished his three years of training. I don't think Forestry Management ever knew he'd been gone.

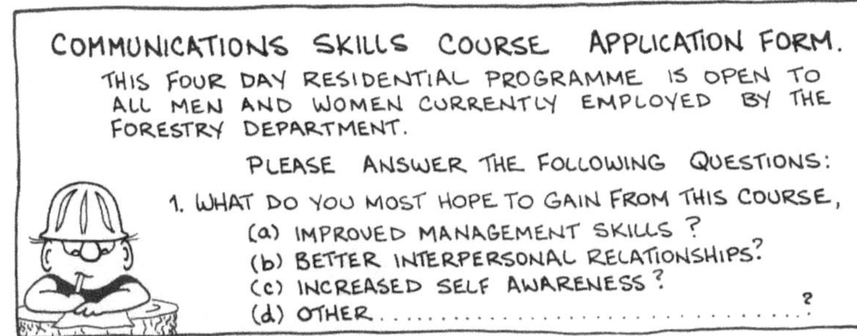

Flange was so nicknamed because his flaccid member was long enough to knock over 6 x 50 cent pieces, stood up edge to edge on a table. He proudly demonstrated this to anyone who would stand still long enough to put the coins out.

Sparrow. Tall and thin with a sparse bit of hair on his chin.

There were many Blues or Blueys, ginger hair of course.

Reverend, because he was forever preaching at us, not religious, just stuff.

Spook, because in the dark you couldn't see him, until he opened his eyes. Or smiled.

Nino was one of our instructors, he had a dodgy knee which would always play up if it was going to rain later that day. His knee always 'knew' when rain wasn't far away, hence KneeKnow.

Lofty was a tall ex Woodsman turned instructor, his favourite pastime was throwing a pinecone or rock at a trainee Woodsman working on the hill, and then pointing at another Woodsman further away, as if that was the culprit, thereby starting a rock or pinecone throwing fight which could go on for quite some time. Fit young men with strong right arms can throw a pinecone a long way, and quite accurately as well. Safety helmets no doubt staved off some of the worst injuries and often one simply ducked the incoming missile. Lofty taught me how to swear, and then when I matured enough to give him back some of his own lip, he wrote in my final report for the year that I was 'Foul mouthed and disrespectful towards instructors'. Try explaining that to your mum next time you go home!!!

I've also seen Lofty waiting till someone was halfway up a tree and then encouraging another Woodie to try cutting it down while you were up there.

Another instructor was 'Swannee', whose apparent only clothing was a Swandri jacket. This garment was worn everywhere, work, play, social events. Maybe he had more than one?

Soapy, Lux, Goober, Duh, Super Duh, Hapuka, Wog, every intake had some amazing names. I only recently learned how Cat Rooter got his name. And you might expect Wog to be something like a gollywog, but no, his Christian names were William Oswald G. And NO, I'm not going to tell you how BigBalls got his name. And it's not what you might think!

# Stories.

Some of the stories from these Woodsman experiences are collected here. There were some fabulously good experiences, and some not so good. We became men.

It should be remembered that all of us 'Are who we are' because of our experiences through life, both the good and the bad, so while some of these experiences were definitely 'Bad' at the time, those of us who lived through the tough times were generally better people for it.

Many of the work ethics were downright dangerous, but it was a different time. Also, many of the practices in the hostels were brutal, barbaric, even criminal, and today one might go to jail for a wide range of things that were then considered normal.

A lot of people, including myself, learned lessons that took years to get over. I personally learned that I could solve all my problems with my fists and for many years that was who I was. It was a defence against being bullied or beaten again. A 'get them before they get me' mentality. Fortunately, I eventually got past that, and I hope everyone else managed their particular demons. Not everyone had problems though, many just went through the system and had a lifetime career doing stuff they loved.

I should probably point out a few things. The various reference books I have read give conflicting data. In one, the number of new Woodsmen in 1971 was 47, but the same book lists 110 as having started. Another book lists our graduation percentage as 28%, but 13 graduating from 110 doesn't equal that figure. (13 from 47 is 28%). My understanding is; The intake in 1971 had 77 new trainee Woodsmen, but because of the hazing / bullying, by March about 30 youngsters had already left. So, another 33 replacements were brought in. At the end of our second year, 13 of us from the 110 graduated from Golden Downs and went on to our third and final year. This was not typical of most new intakes, although I think our 1971 numbers were about the worst ever (11.8% graduation).

Terrible statistics, and I have no idea whether the Forest Service Management were ever taken to task for the appalling dropout rate. Certainly, the management and other forestry staff including hostel managers turned a blind eye to a lot that went on. Some of the bullying was just well meaning, hi-spirited hi-jinks, but much of it went well beyond that. Suffice to say that whatever the real numbers, it was a terrible graduation rate and obviously, hard enough so that most of the lads weren't willing to stay. Records from multiple books record 1149 Woodsmen began at Golden Downs with a total of 534 graduating. Possibly, several hundred went on to further training or transferred to Ranger School, it's a little difficult to tell as the numbers aren't crystal clear. However the numbers are read, it obviously wasn't everybody's dream job. And how many potentially fabulous employees did Forestry loose because of one incident too many which caused someone to quit their dream job?

Physically the work was hard, and it turned soft young schoolboys who didn't have much academic interest, into very fit, strong capable young men. It was a hard life.

I have heard it said that the Woodsman Schools took 'the best of the dumbest'. Light hearted jest for those of us who didn't qualify (academically), for Ranger school, but the reality turned out to be quite different. Those of us who came to the Woodsman system might not have been academically inclined at that age, but with a few years of work experience under our belts, I would consider the Woodsmen I knew to be among the most capable and confident people of anyone I have ever met, many going on to senior management and even academic positions and careers.

As much as possible, in their own words, the following tales come from some of the guys who made the Woodsman Schools their homes.

**Cam Barrowman.**

My first memory of the Woodsman school was a letter arriving in the mail confirming my appointment as a Junior Woodsman at Golden Downs, the letter detailed that I was to be at Bigg's Corner on 12 January 1957. I travelled by New Zealand Road Services bus from Greymouth, stopping at Murchison to take on extra passengers. We were dropped off at Bigg's Corner and I met a group of other lads, all Woodsmen to be.

Introducing ourselves, I met Bill 'Pinetree' R. who had grown up in Murchison, as well as a bunch of other lads. Peter 'Beefy' G., an older Woodsman arrived in a J1 Bedford and drove us all to the hostel where we met the OC and the Matron (Len and Mrs C). Plus about 40 other newly arrived first years (we had 81 in total), and a bunch of 2nd year Woodsmen who were looking us over and awaiting the first opportunity to start our indoctrination. This started on our first night with tippings out of bed, buckets of water thrown in through one's door, the usual sort of rubbish. A few of the more belligerent characters were dragged off to the showers for a bit of argy bargy, pushing around and the odd punching.

Before leaving for the Downs I had fortunately had a bit of heavy work experience at a timber dressing plant in Hokitika, so I was no longer a skinny 16 year old weakling and I was able to 'stand up' to some of the bullying from the bigger second year guys.

Our first job was low and medium pruning, and in the summer months in the hot Nelson sun we were very grateful for the low canopy of the treetops. We were mainly pruning Radiata, the branch sizes were not too large and relatively easy to cut. Much more difficult to prune was the Douglas Fir or Oregon Pine, this species had very unyielding branches, which we had difficulty pushing our way into and through, before we could begin to cut the branches from the tree. There were many pockets and lumps of sticky gum on the branches and tree trunks, which would get all over our hands and clothes, we needed to wash this off with kerosene or petrol at the end of the day. If left on the skin it would turn very hard and black.

We also had some serious exposure to arsenic. Some head office type person decided it would be good to save costs on thinning operations by using poisons and so in a remote radiata block we used the old 'Indian' fire fighting Water Knapsacks. We mixed the arsenic, filled our packs and then used a variety of methods to apply it to the trees. Cutting a notch in the tree, very much like a small scarf and then pumping a bit of arsenic in was the most often used method. It was pretty unworkable as the knapsacks leaked and we all got covered with arsenic. Often we worked all day with small leaks down our backs, but when we had a major spill, maybe got soaked from head to foot in the stuff, we would jump into the nearest pond or creek if one was available. One of our guys, Peter W., got very sick and was hospitalised for many weeks. Our poisoning operations didn't last for long but I'm told that it cropped it's ugly head back up many times during forestry's history. We definitely didn't like that work. I never found out how successful the poisoning was, as years later, Woodies were still axe and chain saw thinning.

One of the memories I treasure was associating with Ray H., (55 intake), the winner of the Corbett Award in his intake. Ray was an exceptional Woodsman and Axeman, and went on not only to found a very successful logging company in the deep south but also achieved fame as a competitive Axeman along with other previous great Axemen from Golden Downs.

Obviously, there was plenty of wood to practice our axeman skills on, and regularly, our thinnings were taken off the hill to be used for competitions. As we came into winter we moved into the planting operations and regularly found ourselves working up high, often in low cloud or snow covered hills. One area to be planted was Long Gully, and parts of this place were so rocky that we had to carry bags of dirt to plant each tree in. So we had a bag of seedlings and a bag of dirt, and when the dirt ran out we would trudge to the nearest place where we could get a refill. Sometimes only feet away, sometimes hundreds of yards.

Often a pig or two would charge out of a gully when we approached, and when that happened we all dropped tools and gave chase. More often than not the pigs won the race, but occasionally, there was fresh pork for the cookhouse.

Our cook was Greasy Jim, his 2 staff were were Josh and Margaret H., and the spaghetti sandwiches they gave us for lunch were truly disgusting. I did get a part time job in the cookhouse with them. After the evening meal I stayed in the cookhouse, washing dishes and helping make the lunches for the next day, so I guess lunches were partly my fault. Eventually, in my 4th year, with the savings I made from working in the cookhouse I was able to buy a 1938 Austin 14.

Mainly our tutors and mentors were 3rd and 4th year Woodies, although we had many instructors who were from the UK and they were on just as big a learning curve as we were.

Mid summer, 1958, and a group of us, myself, Tony S., Alex L., Max E., and Ian D., were low pruning some Laricio Pine in Blow's Block when one of our instructors, Warren E., raced up and told us to bring our gear, we were off to a fire at Sandy Bay, over past Motueka (Marahau). The fire was threatening the Kaiteriteri community and quite a few baches, about 90 k's away. Warren drove the V8 'Saddle Tank' fire engine all the way over to the fire, with a couple of hose packs and a Wajax pump, and with us four Woodsman sitting on top of the tanks, holding onto whatever we could find. As the tanks were quite curved at the edges it's a miracle we never slid off. On approaching the danger area Warren shouted out "better get a bit of lunch boys, we're going to be busy shortly", so we pulled out our cut lunches from inside our shirts, and one handed, we munched on the spaghetti sandwiches as we drove. I recall one of us lost his sandwich which fell into the fire engine's driveshaft and we were all covered with scattered spaghetti and bread. Once there, we put our Woodsman skills into practice, attacked the fire and soon had it out, to the encouragement and good natured jibing from a few locals. We were back at the hostel by about 10.30 pm and I remember the extra pay we got didn't even cover the cost of a crate of DB.

At one time during my third year at the Downs, there were 42 pig dogs kennelled under the stand of Radiata Pine at the south end of the front hostel. Saturday morning, 4.00 am and everyone was trying to get their dogs out and into vehicles for the weekends hunting, it was just bedlam. We were all heading for whatever block we had been allocated; Wai-iti, Long Gully, Beebees Ridge, Blue Glen, Wellington Gully, Blows, Gordons Knob, to name just a small few of the places available to us. Standing in the quiet of the predawn, rifle in hand, dog sitting by your side, slight breeze in the face, listening to the dawn chorus of Bellbird, Tui and Pigeon, was a magic I'll never forget. The Radiata and Muricata Pine plantations were full of Bush Robins, more so when these plots were bounded by Beech or Podocarp mix forests. And then, of course there was the hunting. Not all of my friends were hunters, for some a stag roaring at dawn was just noise, but for me it was the thrill of the hunt, the pleasure of the provider, the ultimate challenge.

In 1959 an Englishman of very slim build and a somewhat nervous disposition joined us at Golden Downs. He was an Etymologist and worked with our local Bug-man, Arthur H. Of course the Englishman became 'the Pom', and it wasn't long before he showed an interest in hunting, which he'd never had the opportunity to do back home. I was asked to take him pig-hunting, and as I'd just been told of a mob of pigs living in a patch of bracken fern surrounding the Beech forest at Long Gully, I thought it was a golden opportunity to get the Pom 'blooded'. We had a high roofed station wagon which was ideal for carting the pig dogs in, and bright and early Saturday morning we put the dogs, the rifles and the Pom (he volunteered, honest), in the back and off we went. The Pom was white before he hopped in the vehicle, you should have seen him when we let him and the dogs out at the start of our hunting block. The dogs were immediately onto some scent and off they went, with us following as best we could. This was the south end of Ridge Road and man, there's some rough country in there. We struggled to keep up with the dogs, when we stopped for a breather the Pom said, "how exciting, I've never done this before". Soon the dogs had bailed several pigs and we managed to catch up. We found them in the bottom of a steep gully, in a patch of Red Beech. The leader of the pigs was a massive black boar and our holder had him by the snout and was being flung about quite a bit. The .303 stopped the pig, all was well except one dog had been opened up at the shoulder by a tusk. We wrapped the dog's wound and carried him back to the vehicle, along with the pig. By the time we were back at the truck the dogs were exhausted and so was the Pom. They all got in the back with the pig and the wounded dog and back home we went. We looked a proper sight getting out off the truck at the Downs, covered in blood and pig and dog hair. I'm sure all Woodie pig hunters will be forever grateful to Mrs K, Cliff's wife, for the surgery and stitching she did on our dogs. This particular pig was sold to the pub in Wakefield, as our cookhouse had plenty that day. The Pom never forgot his first days hunting. I don't think he ever became a hunter but he developed a keen interest in caving.

Going through the Woodsman school was a magic experience for me, there was an 'aura' to Golden Downs that is still strong in my memory today.

About a mile or so east of the Kopara sawmill on the eastern Haupiri River, the water was quite deep in most parts so a river crossing had been set up by installing two heavy steel rope cables, suspended between trees on either side of the river. About 5 feet apart vertically, the lower cable was fitted with a large steel ring about 10 inches in diameter with a chain several yards long and this was attached to the bow of a 16 - 17 foot dinghy. This system had been set up by the sawmill staff to enable access to the other side of the river where there was approximately 3 square miles of Rimu, Kahikatea, Matai, Miro and a mixture of Podocarp forest for the mill to access. The upper cable was to allow people to walk across the lower cable while holding onto the upper one. We regularly used this shortcut, usually with large packs on our backs. We could also cross the river in the dinghy. An experienced person could manipulate or flick the chain and so move the boat from one side of the river to the other.

One Friday afternoon we had a full boat load of Woodsmen and Rangers, all with packs on. Perhaps the boat was a tad overloaded? One of our group was a prankster from Taupo, John 'Tiki' R., who was always ready to entertain, always ready to play a prank or practical joke. He was doing the chain sliding thing, with much more vigour than was required. He would pull the boat close to the main rope and then let it go and as the boat moved back down with the current, he would flick the chain, and of course the boat moved across the river. When he did this vigorously, the boat would surge a bit and we would all get a good shaking. After the 3rd or 4th shaking, one of the Rangers said to me, "move over a bit mate, I'm going to fix that little arsehole". As Tiki was doing his next chain flicking trick, Dick, the Ranger got to Tiki at the same time as the bow of the boat was under the main rope, which was not good and water flowed over the boat which sank in a big rush, leaving us all floundering in about 10 feet of water close to the middle of the river. We all managed to exit our backpacks, and all surfaced OK. We all got to prove that we could swim with boots on, and Tiki learned some new variations of the English language that day.

**Denis Wastney.**

When I came to the Woodsman school in 1957 our introduction (or indoctrination), was to be thrown around while completely wrapped up in blankets. Not knowing where the next push is coming from was scary. Those of us who objected had our balls nuggeted, or smeared with toothpaste, occasionally with a bit of horse liniment added to help us to run faster. Obviously, the second-year guys had to have some way of having fun. Another favourite prank that we had visited upon us was; we would be put into the middle of a blanket held at each corner by four second year guys, who would then bounce us up and around, catching us as we fell. Sometimes some spectacular heights were achieved, especially with the lighter guys. Unfortunately for us, this was done underneath some low hanging power wires and it was scary. Looking back, I don't think we could have reached the power lines, but we didn't know that at the time.

We weren't allowed cars but quite a few of us had pushbikes, so we had races along the corridor to see who could get the fastest time. These time

trials graduated to riding a ramp up onto the pool table at full speed and, when that novelty wore off, the race progressed to doing a hard right hand turn from the pool table to the table tennis table, and then down a down ramp. That had to stop when some bright spark decided to remove the down ramp without the rider knowing about it. One of us went a bit fast, couldn't stop on the table tennis top and went through the big plate glass window at the end of the recreation room. By some fantastic luck, no one was hurt. We were grounded for a month for the window though.

After being threatened with a tipping out of bed, Charlie P. decided to lock his door at night by slipping an axe head under the door, like a wedge. Unfortunately, he hadn't realised that the rest of the crew had caught a live possum earlier in the day which had been slipped under his blankets. The possum, all snug and cosy didn't appreciate being disturbed when Charlie hopped into bed, and Charlie had a great deal of trouble getting the axe out from under the door. The possum eventually escaped into the fireplace in the rec room; it wasn't burning at the time.

One trick used occasionally was to sneak into someone's room and take out the lightbulb and replace it with a sixpence under the terminals. When the Woodie came in and turned on his light, there would be a hell of a bang, the bulb would usually explode, and of course then one had to go find shovel and brush to clean up the glass. As well as ask for a new light bulb. And ask the hostel manager to fix the blown fuse.

Of course, we experimented with making canons. A piece of pipe and something to use as a projectile, a bit of powder out of a rifle cartridge and a homemade wick was enough to get a good bang. Firing anything into the fireplace was deemed to be pretty safe, until one evening the bang was at the wrong end of the pipe, something blew backwards and embedded itself in the wall just beside some guys on the other side of the room. Lots of bad language bouncing around the room that night.

We often made bombs of various sorts to catch the eels or trout in the river. Occasionally a small bomb (often carbide), was thrown into the swimming hole while other Woodies were having a dip after work or on weekends. The looks on people's faces trying to get out of the water hole were priceless, until of course, the trick was played back on you.

We never had much spare cash, our wages were on the slim side, so when the fruit and veggie man from Motupiko came selling his wares, some of the guys would get him talking on one side of his truck while someone else sneaked in on the other side and helped themselves. At the time it seemed like fair game, but maybe not so much now that I'm a bit older and hopefully wiser.

One of our intake had just finished Compulsory Military Training and he brought a rifle to the Downs. He was demonstrating the army procedures in the rec room one night when he accidentally fired a shot. Many rooms had a bullet hole through them until the bullet exited an outside wall. These were hurriedly taped or pictured over. We were super fortunate no one was hurt.

The Downs was near a prime apple, raspberry, hops and tobacco growing area, and of course there were always plenty of seasonal pickers coming to the district. Often dances were held at Tapawera, and this was a great opportunity for young Woodies to go meet some young ladies. Some of us had cars, often stashed in and around the local area and we would cycle to these cars and then travel out and about for socialising activities. Or we would cadge a ride anyhow we could, often hitchhiking. This was usually a good opportunity to try and sneak booze back to the hostel, and the best secret hiding places were in the walls and ceilings. The OC was having a hostel inspection when a particular piece of ceiling collapsed and many bottles of beer fell to the floor, much of it breaking. Of course, no one knew who owned it, but the entire hostel was grounded for a month.

On one jaunt to Nelson, we missed the last bus back to the Downs and so, looking for a bed for the night, we snuck into the cathedral around midnight. Tiki R, who could play an organ, decided to play 'When the Saints come marching in', and after a short musical session, the police came and gave us alternative accommodation for the night. On the occasions when we asked nicely (after missing the bus), we could usually get a bed and a cuppa at the Police Station. Not sure if that would happen today?

Several of the lads happened to have an issue with one particular instructor (Dave S), who was staying in one of the second-year huts for a while. A roll of barbed wire was found and quietly wrapped around his hut while he was inside asleep. Then a dozen or so lads gave the hut a good shaking, rocking it around on its skids to simulate an earthquake. Of course, Dave couldn't get out and as usual, the culprits were never found.

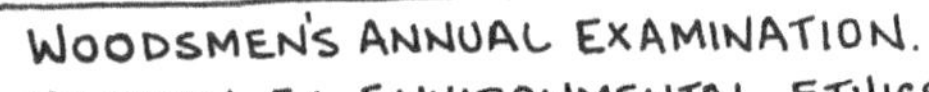


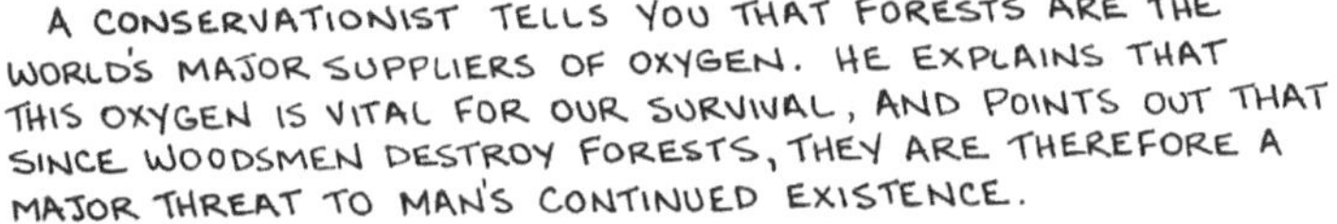

**Mike Bange.**

In 1979 I spent 12 months as a PEP worker (government employment scheme) for the Forest Service in Tairua Forest. The work was physically demanding and probably set me up well for Woodsman Training. We travelled daily from Waihi to Tairua, quite a few of the other guys found it too physically demanding and left, but I was much more challenged by the academic side of things. I had an interview with the Forestry for a position as a trainee Woodsman and when asked what I would do in the coming year I said that I'd probably keep working at Tairua. They must have liked that reply because I was offered the chance to join the Woodsman Training

School at Kaingaroa. I was stoked to 'get in' as I did enjoy the physical work, an office job was never going to work for me.

The Woodsman hostel at Kaingaroa was nicknamed the Pink Palace, it was a very cold old building, and Kaingaroa Forest was also a very cold place. No one could ever figure out why it was painted pink.

My first year started off great, I had a good room with a reasonable view. In March, I was riding my CB400 motorbike into Rotorua along a stretch of road called the '4 ½' (a long straight not far from Kaingaroa Village), when I was overtaken by 2 older Woodies in a Falcon car. They lost control on a slight bend, rolled, and flipped the car. They sprayed me with so much gravel that I lost control of my bike and crashed down a firebreak. I ended up breaking my back in 3 places. The passenger in the car (Pipi), broke a few bones and the Falcon driver came out unscathed. Pipi was a champion surfer; I think he surfed in competitions all over the world. Over the next 3 days I was in 3 different hospitals, over the following 7 weeks I was nursed back to health. Thankfully I healed OK, but due to the time I was away, forestry was talking about me having to 're-do' my entire first year. Eventually they decided that my previous years' work in Tairua would be equivalent to year one at the Woodsman School so that was all good. I had no more incidents in the first year.

Some of the guys I was with were; Nudes (he never wore undies), Slitz who had squinty eyes and JayOne who owned a Bedford truck. Many nicknames were used in different years, there were many intakes who had an Aussie, a Smiler, a Spider. We had a Fat Albert and a Tock. With the new intake in 1981 there were a few keen fishermen, so fishing the Rangitikei River for trout was a favourite pastime. None of us had licences. I caught a lovely brown trout and the hostel manager said "I'll cook that for you boyo", and he did. Some of us decided to try a tube trip down the Rangitikei. We had no idea what to expect from the rapids, but we were young fit and keen for adventure so a few bruises were a small price to pay. The trip down to Murupara took a few hours but we all made it ok.

There was a big concrete water tank in the village, about 80 feet high. A handful of us boys climbed up to the top and decided to abseil down. I clipped the carabiner onto the rope and went over the edge, only to have the carabiner become unclipped. I was very lucky I was holding on to both ropes, otherwise I wouldn't be here now. I pulled myself back up to the top and climbed down the ladder. That was a close shave.

We did a lot of drinking, regular trips to the Waiatapu pub, and as often as not we made the trip home with stolen souvenirs, handles and glasses. We went to Ruapehu for a cheap fun day, sliding down the hill on black plastic bags. Of course the bottles of beer we had hidden under our swannies soon spilled or broke and we stunk of booze. We did have sober drivers for that trip. For a time I had a CA Bedford which had sliding doors for both driver and passenger. One day the boys decided it needed a new paint job, so they got a few different coloured paint bombs (spray paint cans), from the Forestry store and proceeded to paint different band names all over the van. That made it pretty unique.

The Kaingaroa hostel had many leaks and when it rained heavily, the fire alarms would often go off. That was a real pain in the middle of the night. We had a canteen that we could buy snacks from. Our cookhouse provided great food. We all had to do a two week stint, learning life skills in cookery and food preparation. The last day of our two year training was a big celebration for two reasons; we were the last ever intake into the Woodsman training at the Kaingaroa hostel. The hostel burned down not long after we left. The first year guys that still had one year of training to go were transferred to Golden Downs to finish their second year, before being transferred to various forests to complete their third year.

The final dinner in the cook house was a treat. Special food, puddings, cake. No one was eating much, so the head chef walked up to the cake casually cutting a large slice from it and looked around and threw it. That started the biggest food fight in history, what a mess but bloody good fun. There was a mini tanker of beer on the final day with the OC in attendance. We had completed two of our three years and we were now off to the big wide world to follow our dreams of making it big. I got transferred to Reefton on the West Coast of the South Island for my final year. I had an awesome year and I got my Woodsman certificate at the end of the year.

**Reid Mallinson.**

After a couple of hard weeks work doing forestry stuff at Golden Downs forest our Friday excursion was keenly looked forward to. Pre-departure before getting on the bus entailed some careful preparation of one's presentation; Bodgie clothes, Beatle suits, winkle picker shoes etc., and copious amounts of 'Brylcream' to carefully shape the 'ducks arse' in the hair on the back of the head. The lengths one went to when going 'Dear' hunting!

Once the bus had departed, the jovial atmosphere was bolstered by a sing along featuring the songs of the day such as Ten Guitars and Cotton Fields etc., normally heaps of volume with bugger all rhythm.

In Nelson, we all split up doing our own thing, but would quite often congregate again at the upstairs night spot called the Picalo Paradiso, where the local radio station broadcast live, the music of the day, and the dance floor was full of gyrating young people doing the twist and stomp. One would have to say though, that the Woodsmen's dancing more resembled grubber planting, release cutting, axe thinning and low pruning all rolled into one!

I remember one night a couple of us missed the bus back to the Downs, and back in those days it wasn't acceptable to sleep on the streets, so what to do? On our search late at night for lodging options we came across a ladder almost down to the footpath outside a hotel. This might work? Looking around over our shoulders we made a unanimous decision and scarpered up to an open window and there we were in a vacant flash hotel room. This'll do mate, sheer luxury for us Woodsmen, so we hit the sack and crashed out. In the morning we were suddenly woken by a knock on the door. "Oh shit, we've been caught". But then a lady pleasantly said, "Are you awake? I have your morning cup of tea", "Oh yes Ma'am, that would be lovely, thank you Ma'am". So there we were, free lodging, a morning cup of tea and then a sneaky little escape from the pub!

Feeling a little guilty I did go back several times and pay for a few drinks to make up for that indiscretion!

## Karamea.

I came to the Downs (Golden Downs Woodsman School) as a very quiet conservative 16-year-old. I hadn't done well in my School Certificate exams (I barely scraped a pass in English and Maths with 50% in both). I guess most of us were well out of our depth, most having just left school.

My first vivid memory is meeting several other new Woodies at the main road entrance to the Downs (Bigg's Corner), where we were dropped off

by the NZ Railways Road Services bus. 'Fats' wasn't impressed when I offered him a cigarette from my gold-plated cigarette case which was a leaving home present from my parents.

My second vivid memory is at the welcoming introduction, the OC (Officer in Charge), Tug W., telling the assembled group of new first years that he wasn't going to call me by a 'poofy' name such as mine and he would call me 'Harry'. So that became my nickname, for life.

Memory 3 is; on about my third or fourth night at the Downs, being tipped out of bed at three in the morning. Obviously, a huge shock, also, it hurt. Having the wire frame bed on top of my head wasn't good. It also scared the shit out of me. After several weeks and the third time of being tipped out of bed (we couldn't lock our doors), I was almost too scared to sleep at night. So, when I heard the second-year guys tiptoeing down the corridor in the middle of the night whispering to each other, I got out of bed and hid behind the door. Sure enough, at a given signal, a corridor full of the second-year guys crashed the doors open, ran in, upended the bed, then ran back across the hallway to do the same to the new Woodie on the other side of the corridor. Then, sounding like bedlam, all those sets of feet charging down the corridor, yahooing, laughing and creating an almighty din, and then they went back to their own rooms. What a din. Only this time, I was hiding behind my door, and as my assailant exited my room, my fist 'sort of' contacted his nose. A few minutes later, as I was putting my bed back together, 5 or 6 of the second-year guys came for me, dragged me to the ablution block, put me under a cold shower, gave me a punch or two, tore my pj's to shreds, and then took me out to the rugby field where they chained me (naked, arms spread), to the goal posts. Matron Kay (Mrs M), found me there at 6.00 am when she came to work. Needless to say, she wasn't happy, I wasn't happy. I wasn't really physically harmed, but…??

At the recent (2023) Reunion I had one of my second-year guys (Jawbone), tell me he was one of the lads who dealt to me that night. Which is cool, I have never remembered who took me to the showers. For me, there are no hard feelings, I don't think there ever were, it just changed my way of thinking. A bonus from this standing up for myself / shower / beating / chaining, was that I was never again touched or bullied by any second year, I was never again harassed.

A memory which has always thrilled me was some of my time spent in my 3rd year as a worker in the Fire Station. At the end of our second year, we were expected to pick a forest somewhere else in NZ and go there for our third year, usually for a specialty career learning path which wasn't available in the Nelson / Golden Downs facility. I chose to stay in Golden Downs for the fire season (through summer), and I worked exclusively at the fire station. Along with several other 3rd and 4th year Woodies, (Whitey, Fats, Sparrow and Spooner), our tasks were generally driving the fire engines on patrol around the entire forest; putting out fires started by tourists who had stopped and were boiling the billy on the side of the road. Keeping an eye out for smoke, going to the various work sites and making sure there were no sparks from chain saws or other machinery. Ensuring that spark arrestors on log skidders, bulldozers, saws etc., were fitted and being used.

That summer (1973), was particularly hot and dry and for a few weeks the fire danger was so high that logging crews were starting work under flood lights at 2.00 am and finishing for the day at 10 am. I have seen trees with the bark 'blown off' due to the sap underneath getting so hot that the tree exploded.

As part of the fire crew, I also worked on fire control work, using fire as a tool to prepare new blocks of land for re-planting after logging operations were complete. Lighting fires can be hard work, and there are many ways to get fires going quickly and efficiently. Firebreaks and tracks are easiest because one can walk on foot with a burning flame wand and just stick the flame in the gorse or fern. On suitable roads or tracks, Fire engines or trucks with a flame thrower unit attached, can send out a plume of high-pressure burning diesel, and everything in its path get set ablaze. Decent flame throwers are fun, but also hot, hard work.

One of the coolest ways of getting a fire going in rough terrain was throwing napalm bombs out of a helicopter. This method is only used when the perimeter of a controlled burn is inaccessible to vehicles, or perhaps unsuitable for pedestrian access. Or perhaps, if Management want a fire started somewhere else where vehicle or foot access isn't possible, ie., a slash filled gully in the centre of the block. I remember sitting in the fire station all week making petrol bombs. Filling a plastic bag with petrol, adding a spoon or two of petrogel, adding fuse and detonator, tying the bag

shut and giving it a good shake to mix the components, which then sets to a 'jelly like' consistency. Then stacking all the 'bombs' in boxes. We made many hundreds, maybe thousands of these. Then, when the time was right, conditions were good, Management said "Go", off we went to light our fire. The block to be burned could be thousands of acres, generally it had been surrounded by firebreaks, bulldozed tracks, and other bare land.

The Fire Controller co-ordinated dozens or hundreds of people to light the fire, which is a science in itself. Woodsman with portable flame throwers on their backs, or a fire wand in hand, would walk the perimeter, fire engines and other vehicles with bigger flame throwers would drive appropriate roads and, where the terrain was too inhospitable, helicopters would fly the perimeter with a worker throwing prepped bombs out the door. I doubt Health and Safety would allow such practices these days. I mean, imagine a helicopter stacked to the gunnels with petrol bombs!!! Generally, the fuses were lit with cigarettes, the bomb thrown out the door or just dropped onto the ground below. When the 'bomb' ignited, the burning napalm stuck to anything below, wood / shrubs / trees / gorse / fern, and of course, this was a great way to get a perimeter burning. Good fun too. Brings out the latent arsonist in the best of us. Who doesn't like watching a good fire?

As enjoyable as this work was, I have spent many hundreds of hours fighting forest and other fires, and the devastation and heartbreak is something that stays with you forever. Seeing and hearing fauna (kiwi, possums, pigs), being destroyed by fire is heartbreaking. My heart always goes out to the people in other parts of the world (Australia, California, Spain, Greece in recent times), when their summer season arrives, and they suffer this horror annually.

While on Fire Crew at the Downs, a group of us had money only for either beer or food until next payday, so we decided to round up a couple of wild sheep so as not to completely starve. Fats had a Humber 80 with a roof rack on it, so being the intrepid hunters we were, and deciding to hunt in comfort, we put a mattress on top of the roof rack and two of the guys sat up there with rifles, while the other two sat in the car, one spotlighting and one driving. Near Tapawera there was a single lane bridge that was more like a double ended ramp than a bridge, and unfortunately Fats took this hump in true speed racer fashion. None of us had twigged that the two struts holding the roof rack on were designed for very light loads, and upon landing the car after the bridge jump, the struts broke, the roof rack, mattress, Woodsmen, guns and all, slid down off the roof, over the bonnet, neatly depositing said Woodsmen, guns and mattress on the ground. Fats managed to stop without running any of us over, but it was a close call. No shots were fired, but the bonnet of the Humber was never quite right again and it had several large parallel groves across it. We didn't get any sheep either.

Part of the Woodsman experience was to work at one of the popular walking tracks, often the Wangapeka or Heaphy tracks, for track cutting experience, but there was a lot more involved than just putting in new tracks. Building new wire rope swing bridges, repairing or building new huts, pest control work, was all part of the job, and each involves some awesome skills. Blasting rocks, working with horses, boats, saws, helicopters, they were all just part of everyday life. Visitors today to the Karamea Limestone Arch, the Heaphy, and all other New Zealand tracks are walking on tracks dug and blasted from the hills and rock faces by Woodsman from the various schools.

Building a new swing bridge for example. First the country must be surveyed, to decide where the bridge is going to be. Then a light line must be got from one side of the ravine / gully / crevasse to the other. Abseiling is a useful skill. This light line is then used to pull heavier ropes across, and these are used to pull across heavy wire cables. These are then anchored to bolts drilled and concreted into the rocks. Or possibly, other suitable anchor points such as concrete slabs need to be made. Making framework or boxing for cement constructions in the middle of the bush can take a bit of doing. Including carrying the bags of cement and builders mix / sand to the site. Luxuries such as helicopters aren't always available, especially when one has cheap Woodie labour on hand. Water for the concrete has to be brought up from the creek or river and then one needs something to mix the concrete in. Once the main cables are in place, then, starting from each side of the bridge, a Woodsman (expendable??) sits on the 4 or 5 deck cables and installs the tread plates. These plates keep the cables at the correct spacing and distance from each other. We eventually meet in the middle, and we now have a flexible walkway across the chasm. Side ropes and handrails follow, with guy wires, stays and stabilisers, which all work to stop excessive sway. We tied ourselves on and tools were always tied on to our hands, but in those days, we didn't have fall arrestors or body harnesses. They may have existed, but we certainly didn't have them.

One of my instructors on the Heaphy Track was a guy I'll call Pete D.V. Pete was always looking for more interesting ways of doing things. When hunting deer became too tame for him, he swapped to using a crossbow for hunting, and when that became too tame he started sitting up in a tree waiting with a knife. He had some interesting experiences from that particular activity, he's been stuck by antlers a time or two, but he got what he wanted.

Pete was great practical joker and once, while creating the track to the Limestone Arch in Karamea we were drilling holes to blast a big rock to pieces. Once the holes were filled with gelignite, Pete would install the fuses and then send us Woodies to wait at a safe zone away down the track. He would light the fuses, then come back and join us while we waited for the bang. On one occasion we waited and waited, but Pete didn't join us, and there was no bang. Then we heard Pete's voice in the distance calling us back. As we rounded the corner to the blast site we saw a piece of fuse stuck in the bank, burning and we all ran in every direction, some straight over the edge of the bank, some back, some forward. To the sound of Pete's hilarious laughter. It was just a piece of burning fuse, attached to nothing, just stuck in the bank. Ha Ha, very funny, thanks Pete.

In the mid 70's there was a big storm in the Tasman and a Japanese fishing boat was abandoned by its crew. Once the weather had settled, Pete decided to swim to the abandoned ship, take possession (under his understanding of maritime salvage law), and then 'on sell' the ship to the

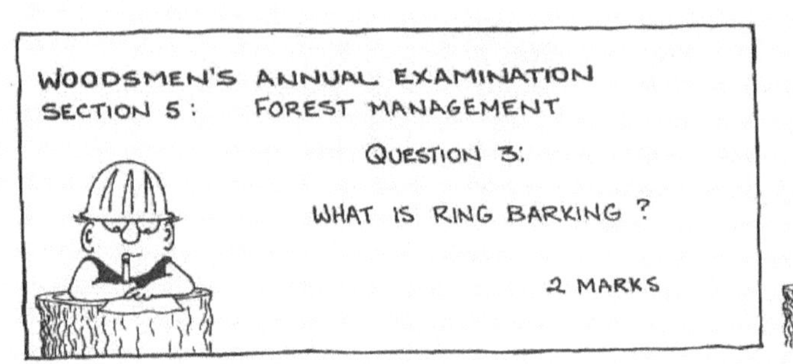

highest bidder. After some weeks of no action or results, Forestry Management radioed Pete on board the ship and told him in no uncertain terms to get back to the Woodsmen trainees that he'd abandoned or lose his job. He did come back to work quite the hero. And the Japanese fishermen got their boat back unharmed and at no cost.

I've always been most impressed with words of wisdom that I got from more than one of my instructors; Be observant, spot danger before it finds you, find the best and easiest way to get the job done safely. Remember your #8 wire mentality, there's always more than one way to get a job done, the fastest isn't always the best.

## Greg Heaven.

My father encouraged me to join the Forest Service. My oldest brother Dennis (Slobs), was already there, and Dad was keen to get me out of the house at the tender age of 15, so sometime in late 1973, I applied for the Woody school and was successful. I thought I might have a better chance if I said I played rugby and cricket but actually, I didn't play either. In my case, 3 years secondary education was enough. I also applied at the same time for a job in the Ministry of Transport but found I was 4 months too young for the MoT.

On the 21st January 1974 I arrived at Golden Downs in my trusty Austin A50, knowing full well we weren't allowed vehicles until 6 months were up. I had broken down my pushbike (no racks in those days), with the intention to leave my car at Quinnies Bush and bike back and forth. That plan failed, I was found out and got slapped on the hand, some guys got away with it, I didn't. That didn't bode too well for the start of my Forest Service career.

Some boys left within the first few weeks as the life was too hard. In the first year we covered all the basic training. I think of all the pruning lifts, axe thinning, slasher thinning, chainsaw thinning, with cotton wool for ear plugs and overalls. I recall thinning in a real hairy block of Pine trees with

Echo chainsaws, the rainwater was running down my back after making it past my bush helmet, then proceeding down my crack and onto my legs. How thrilling was that?

I also recall standing with my right foot on a log and resting my chainsaw on my thigh while checking the path to my next tree. In a few seconds I had a classic steam burn on my inner thigh, from the saw's exhaust. I jumped and made good use of some of the gutter language which we all learnt whilst at Woody school. I sustained a well outlined burn on the skin that took many weeks to heal.

While slasher thinning we came across a wasps nest. Hence yours truly received some stings, at which, to the delight of many, the other blokes proceeded to use the flat side of their heavy slashers on my head, squashing any remaining critters. Thanks guys (I've probably never been quite right in the head ever since).

Planting time (Pinus Radiata), was hard yakka. We were normally given the grottiest blocks to plant, we were lucky to plant 300 – 400 trees a day. On the steep open country it was not uncommon for gourlies (large rocks), of various sizes to begin rolling downhill, set on their journey by some Instructor or Woody above you on the hill.

As you were working your way uphill planting trees, then suddenly finding one or more gourlies heading your way was a highly entertaining way of livening up the day and getting quite a few laughs from those who weren't in the path of the rocks. Thankfully no one was ever killed.

Poling (where two poles were set in a row to give planters a line to plant to), was a safer option work-wise, as you tended to be working away from the planters with a much smaller group of guys. Also when you were at the top of a hill you were much safer.

It wasn't unknown to light a wee fire during those bloody cold winter days and heat up our chunder pack (lunch), sammies in our alloy toasty pie machine. Cookhouse lunches were made up 24 hours before we got to sample them. While those good ladies in the cookhouse did what they could, with what they had, it was a wonder we survived. We had competitions to see how many baked beans we had in our square white bread wedges, if you got 8 beans you were doing well. The slices of tomatoes were so thin that you could read the newspaper through them. They were not only pale and thin they were pretty tasteless. Cake if we got it was almost inedible and fruit was very rare. I remember my brother Slobs (now Slobs senior), telling me he remembered being dished up dehydrated spud with his meals, that was two years prior to me starting in 1974. I guessed the cooks had to make a living as well and possibly didn't understand that these young men / boys were still growing. They were generally well fed at home and coming to the hard work of forestry, were now expected to carry out hard toil on very limited rations in their first few years. It took me a long time to realise the service (bless em), got more than their pound of flesh out of most of us.

From the early start we were all given nick names, mainly by and from our second years if I recall correctly. I don't know what I would have been called if my older brother as mentioned wasn't called 'Slobs'.

He was a 1972 intake, for 12 months before shifting onto Ranger School in Rotorua. Hence, "You are Slobs' brother aren't you"?

A good number of nicknames weren't too flattering, eventually one accepted it, maybe it even got to the point where you almost forgot your real name.

Most of us were of the era of long hair and bell bottoms, alcohol was banned in camp (understandably), and it wasn't too long before we found secret hideaways behind the drawers of our tallboys. Holes cut in the wall to stash bottles of beer, up in the top of the wardrobes, and in the ceilings were other places from previous intakes. Friday nights were our opportunity to head into town on the old Wadsworth bus, from Tapawera I guess, and travel into Nelson. As I recall, at our introduction speech from Woodsman School OC Tug W., who said "We were the cream of the crop", meaning; 'now behave yourself boys when you are in Nelson'. He possibly gave that speech to each intake to help make his life a little happier, not that it always worked. So us fellas would either go to the pictures and do a bit of shopping with what spare pocket money we might have left, or hit the pubs. Being now 16 and 17 year olds we were still under age, a few of us frequented an old pub and sat in the corner out of sight of the door quietly drinking too much. Then leaving with extra beer for the bus trip home. The trip was around half an hour or so, requiring an essential stop near halfway for a 'wee wee'. We would break into song, "The Golden Downs boys are back on the piss again" and repeated to alert the driver to stop where he could. We would all pile out and depending on the time of evening would piddle up against the bus or ditch or nearby fence. So by the time we arrived back at camp we were mostly quite drunk. The camp Sergeant would welcome us back and inspect our bags on alighting, hence alcohol probably came into camp only after we were allowed to own or use cars (after 6 months).

Hostel life was pretty fair I guess. Most of us quieter ones had the usual kangaroo court for imagined misdemeanours, followed by wire brushing of the head, or being tipped out of your bed in the wee hours of the morning. Being jammed up against the back wall, running the gauntlet down the hallway treatment, and many other stories. We all got the treatment, we were all picked on one way or another. I guess not being a crawler made me an easy target. Hostel duties were part of our training in the first-year, mopping and polishing the hallways, dining area, toilets etc. Other training and skills learned were; quality control work, basically putting in plots 80 by 4 metres in size to assess stems (trees) per hectare, quality of work and for payment purposes. Firearm safety, working in the fire station where I met John B., Jeff H., and Jim S., all great blokes, even, dare I say it, ‘Legends’. I did one of Jim’s experiments using a Bell Helicopter up on Wai-iti Ridge with little dams and a monsoon bucket.

We learned radio procedures, doing test calls to the office (HQ), from all the fire appliances and the ambulance. Little did I know these skills after the Forest Service ended in 1987 would be very useful in my next job. During my second year we moved down to the new Tapawera camp, late in 1974. Before we moved, we used to travel to Tap for our dinner at night in the new cookhouse, prior to shifting down permanently, showering at the Downs before going to dinner. Life in the new camp now as 2nd years wasn’t much different except we were now living in long rows of single units connected together with attached ablutions. We had a Recreation room, a cookhouse, and Matrons room. We would take our bottom sheet and pillow case off for changing once a week, the top sheet dropped down to the bottom and the fresh sheet placed on the top. I can remember Matron (one of our Instructor’s wives), on one occasion during the process of changing my sheet etc., would complain and say “why don’t you buy a hair dryer”, as my hair was still damp after showering. I would never have lived it down if one of the chaps caught me using one. I quickly learned to thoroughly towel dry my hair. That was a great lesson.

Often on the weekends, I used to travel up to Wangapeka to a farm which helped me keep my sanity and keep me out of trouble. John and Shirley R. were like parents to me, I trotted out (dated), their eldest daughter Susan

after meeting her at the Druids Hall dance in Tapawera. Susan had a sister Sandy and 3 younger brothers. They were all good company and helped where they could on the farm, Shirley also fed me well for doing my bit of farm work.

Control burn offs for us Woodies was to stand about 40 metres apart along fire breaks, looking away from the area being treated (burnt), on watch for any fire that may have occurred outside the containment / burn area. I recall on one occasion (I think Peter E. may have been OC fire), you could hear pigs squealing down the gully which prompted looking in that direction. One little piglet ran out and had serious burns. On capturing it I gave it to John B. who promptly put it in a locker of the International Fire Engine, never to be seen again. John later said it died of its wounds. I can recall climbing up to the fork of a beech tree with a 20L Regal Knapsack (water sprayer backpack), to extinguish some burning material, that was quite a challenge. I have to say, burn offs were the best form of fire training. They continued for many years. I found night burning quite spectacular and we did have the odd escapee (fire jump).

I can remember doing a fencing job down from the old camp on the true right of the Motueka river, most of the fence ran parallel to a road and the river was shingle and rocky, digging holes for posts was pretty much impossible. Coming from semi farming stock I had some idea what I was doing, including being used as a crane with one fellow on each of my legs, being lowered down a hole, head under water and wedging out some big rocks.

I was not impressed when it came to term reports, I managed an 'E' which caused more colourful language. We played a friendly game of cricket in Murchison, I was out after about 3 balls.

Release cutting with slashers, in pig fern above your head, in stinking hot weather amongst the fern, dust, sweat and garked (serious scratches), legs was not what one appreciated. We learned to adapt to the extremes of forestry work and life. Not all instructors were cut from the same cloth. During the years that the Woodsman Schools ran, there were some pretty colourful characters. I recollect on one occasion, myself and 3 other

Woodies, whilst travelling back to Tapawera in the TK Beddy (Bedford gang bus), dropped our shorts and daks, standing up on the backseat and giving our loveable instructor 'Scratcher' 4 brown eyes. That went down a treat for us.

Logging in the Douglas Fir with Bob G. was a highlight. I believe reading somewhere that the last planting of Douglas Firs was in 2003. I thought that was a pretty backward step.

A trip up the Marlborough Sounds was organised, about 14 of us Woodies boarded a charter fishing trip. Vast amounts of alcohol were taken on board. Godfrey had a swim overboard with the barracuda, and thankfully survived. A reasonable amount of fish were caught. We had a great weekend.

I recall the experimental workshops (as we called it), being built. Climbing up on the roof to pace out how long it was. The things you did when you were bored. Eventually, all the old Golden Downs workshop operations were shifted to Tapawera. A new Fire Station, pretty flash as well, was now contracted to Fire and Emergency New Zealand.

At the end of the 2nd year or just prior, we were advised to apply for a 3rd year forest to continue our training. O'Reilly, Seddon, Cat Rooter, Radials and myself applied for Eyrewell Forest in Canterbury. We arrived after some time and had to sterilise our vehicles, as they didn't want Dothastroma Pini (a needle blight disease), in Eyrewell Forest. Much of the work in Eyrewell included log salvage, after the August 1975 wind throw, in which much of the forest was flattened. I thoroughly enjoyed that job, but it was dangerous work.

Seddon got injured, with his legs being trapped between 2 logs. He was cutting off uprooted stumps / trees. Many broken bones and lots of very severe bruising. Seddon married the Officer in Charge's stepdaughter, they lived in the village at Eyrewell. Two or three of us did 3 months at Balmoral Forest in 1976, still with timber recovery from the wind throw, including a lot of timber scaling (measuring). There were more injuries, but some fun also. I remember stapling Cat Rooter's overalls to the floor of a hut, while he was in them. Some of our 2nd years were at Eyrewell and Balmoral Forests along with many other Woodies and Rangers etc. I found great difficulty working on the flat stony ground, which prompted me to shift to the Otago Coast Forest, 30 minutes South of Dunedin. I was now a Skilled, and then a Leading Woodsman. Most of the work involved land preparation prior to planting, with supervisory roles, and quality control work which I really enjoyed. Two of us, an ex-Berwick Woodie and I used a KDL Bedford for travelling around the forest putting in trial plots. Then later we had a a Suzuki 4 x 4 L50 2-seater. The forest headquarters; Village, Camp and Fire Station, were based at Taieri Mouth and I managed the Fire Station at Taieri Mouth for a season. I spent 5 years in a single man's hut, with the sea coast on one side and the hills and trees on the other, what a beautiful location.

My work was very varied, and included; Pre Assessment work before Logging, Planting, Quality Control, Burn offs, Wildfires and Standby Duty in case of fires. I cobbered up with wage worker Lester B, who was son of George and Sylvia B, ex Golden Downs Woodsman School Officer in Charge. Lester died after leaving the Forest Service in a parachuting accident in the Taieri river. That was a very sad day, I lost a good mate. I did a stint at Rankleburn, as acting 2IC, and I also supervised the first women's pruning gangs, planting gangs, etc.

I applied for a number of Foreman positions around the country and in 1981, I shifted to Otautau Longwood Forest, Westland / Southland. I was now married with one son, Ben who was born in Winton. I continued similar work, supervising Winter Employment gangs.

It was always good to have an Officer in Charge who liked Woodies, because not everyone did. We had plenty of Woodsmen, ex Woodsmen and blokes from the Ranger schools. The new Isuzu 4 x 4 Fire appliances were being phased in, we were shown how to use them but then interestingly, we weren't allowed to use them. We found that quite amazing.

We did many 'Time and Motion' studies and also investigated new planting techniques, pruning techniques, especially pole pruning with long poles above 6m to obtain an extra 2m bolt (clear wood). Many other experimental activities were carried out.

While at Otautau doing MARVL assessments, (method of assessment of recoverable volume by log type), basically measuring trees for future logging operations, I had a young chap Dean working with me as a wage worker. An amazing, delightful chap, he was always very conscientious. His parents were killed in the Mt Erebus Air crash which was a very sad time in Otautau, for Dean and his entire forestry family.

I lived up in the O/C's house on Snobs hill and when the OC (Ian W and wife Bev) were leaving, I had to vacate. Ian and Bev had bought their own home about 4 doors or so towards town from where we had been living. We were shifted and rented the Ministry of Agriculture and Fisheries house for about 12 months. I applied for the 2nd IC position at Ashley Forest Ranger Training School in North Canterbury. So my wife and Ben and I packed up and moved to Ashley. The interview for the job was done in the Conservancy Office, Christchurch, by Jim H. my ex Otago Coast Forest

O/C. I was told that he didn't like Woodsman, Ranger trainees or Foresters, and that he was now the Ashley O/C. On waiting outside in the foyer for my interview, I could hear Jim's voice saying, "I know Greg", so you chaps will have to ask all the questions. I was ushered in and introduced to the other gentlemen. Ron H, Ranger trainee O/C and Forester, Peter W. Well it ended up with Jim asking most of the questions and half pie answering them for me. It was an amazing interview, a far cry from how it's done today. I still don't know how I got the job. I guess Ian W. must have put in some good words for me.

The Ranger School was totally different and very rewarding. We had two more sons later, Sam and Dean who were born at the Rangiora Maternity home. Ashley Forest was a rugged training forest. Probably one of the dirtiest forests in terms of rubbish undergrowth I had ever worked in. It seemed as if it was designed to make or break you. Different aspects of the Ranger training was similar to Woody training but didn't last as long. That job lasted for about 2.5 years for me. The 'Green Book' * came out, I found and applied for 22 jobs around the country. We did wonder if they had already sorted out the people they wanted to keep to transition to Timberlands? By the 30th April 1987 the Labour Government of the day ended the NZ Forest Service. Many decades of history, life, memories, villages, camps, careers and communities finished. I stayed on for another

* *Note. The Green Book was a document listing all the newly available jobs in the Department of Conservation, prior to all of the forestry employees being sacked.*

3 months in the Forestry house until it became apparent that I was no longer welcome. I shifted to Rangiora, my first own home, and lived there for almost 5 years before divorcing.

I then started up with Department of Conservation as a Fire Depot Wage Worker, and was made redundant after 1 year and 1 week. I then became Scheme Supervisor for the Conservation Corporation at the Kaiapoi Pa site for about 12 months. I found another Forest Service chap to carry that on and around 1990 I went back to working with the Department of Conservation at the Fire Depot in Rangiora, where I spent the next 28 years.

I met Linda in 2007 through Scouting, she has 3 boys as well, so all of our 6 boys attended Scouts. I have been the Group leader for the Rangiora Scout Group for the past 25 years and am currently writing a book on the Scout groups history.

Some of my other interests include tramping the great walks and anything in between, veggie gardening big time. I love it, and spending time with family.

I became a NZQA accredited assessor. I do heaps of equipment inspections throughout Canterbury and the West Coast. While at the Department of Conservation I attended National Fire Officer's workshops throughout NZ. I have worked with the best fire guys in the country.

Part of the job is testing and maintaining hundreds of thousands of meters of rural fire hose. I have serviced innumerable fire pumps and equipment. I worked under the late Roy K. until he was forcibly retired. We attended many fires, completing the mop ups (ensuring the fire is completely out), and later in many support roles. I helped design a Supply Unit (equipment required at fire), a Command Unit (a portacom trailer on twin axles for incident control operations), a Hino Fire appliance along with Bruce J. and Paul F., only 2 were made in NZ.

I have attended and fought fires all over the South Island and also in Victoria, Australia. In 2006 was I was injured, a serious back injury. One third of our contingent to Oz got burned and I still carry the pain of a lower back injury today. Over the years I have received many qualifications and awards.

Fire and Emergency New Zealand (FENZ) came along in 2016. This was another worrying time of life; I continued with the Department of Conservation now charging FENZ for all work carried out. In October 2018 I was appointed as a Depot Technician, I believe all Depot staff were called Technicians by FENZ. My title and operational status was removed. I am now retired, after 48 years on the job, at the age of 65.

I now see life as more important than working.

**Lindsay Arthur's Tale.**

When I left school in August 1960, the New Zealand Forest Service had not long set up a permanent base in Owaka called Eastern District of Southland Conservancy. I gained employment there as a junior labourer, and at some point I became aware of the Golden Downs Woodsman Training Scheme and I applied. I went to Dunedin by steam train for an interview and was accepted, but as I would arrive well after the commencement of the 1961 intake, I declined to go, but left my name in for the 1962 intake.

During the year of 1961, I worked around Owaka on timber cruising, track cutting, planting and by chance, I got to attend a couple of scrub fires. That was very hard work but I loved it. When work was slow in our area, I was posted off to work at Pebbly Hills and Slopedown Forests.

Late in 1961 I was again advised that I had been accepted for the Woodsman scheme and in January 1962 I was off to Nelson to work in Golden Downs for two years. I travelled to Christchurch by train and then by Newman's bus to Nelson. There were about 20 of us on the same bus and we soon worked out that we were all headed for the same place. It was a great adventure for all of us, but for me particularly, as I had never been away from home for more than about three weeks. We arrived at Bigg's Corner in the late afternoon and then onto the Golden Downs hostels. I was placed in the front hostel and we all had separate rooms. Our intake was made up of 48 individuals from mostly the South Island with a small number from the North Island.

So started a whole new life of working in the bush for all of us. A life that I followed until I retired in June 2007. Forestry was quite an unforgiving way of life, great chaps, great mates, but everyone was quickly pulled into line or knocked about for the smallest mistake. The same rules also for any stupidity, and earlier on there was plenty of stupidity. The whole Woodsman cadet scheme was a type of very hands-on and cheap labour. For the most part, training was the simplest basic Forestry processes, but quite regimented as the culture and the work quickly weeded out the unsuitable or less popular guys who didn’t, or couldn’t, adapt to the outdoor life. As I recall, about 10 guys had left before the end of the first week.

Our first work was low pruning Douglas Fir on Kings Ridge. I do remember that I personally had no idea of what sustained hard work was, especially so with an instructor looking over your shoulder. Some of the boys were into it and were soon well ahead of us more useless ones, the good ones were showing up already. Our next job was release cutting on Reay’s Saddle, we were completely exposed to the hot Nelson summer sun, no one knew anything about dehydration. In fact none of us even knew there was such a word. It was a sharp learning curve, we sweated it out heaps. The work was great and the nightly hostel life for the first couple of months was quite hectic, to say the least. Everyone at times was tipped out of bed, or had their balls nuggeted. Some had their hair cut into a mohawk style. Bert, our Welfare Officer was quite a nice person but between us all, we continually ran him ragged every night. Some of us must've taken more than six months to show the slightest sign of maturity.

Our intake had two different cookhouse owners, the first year was not great but in our second year we had a guy called Cliff who we all regarded as being a good guy. Cliff was good to all, sometimes taking a few of us with him on trips out of the Downs. One weekend I remember going to Churtsey, in mid Canterbury, to look at a race horse, and then on the way back, going to the Rangiora races. It was a long trip but a very welcome change from our normal weekends.

Another interesting aspect of Golden Downs was that there was a little general canteen type shop which was managed on a cooperative business style. For every purchase each customer was issued with a docket. These were collected and at the end of each month, they were handed back to the canteen management who totalled them. All the profits were then divided up on a pro-rata basis and credited back to each customer. Management was made up of Forest Rangers and Admin staff. It was a fabulous system which is seldom remembered now, but it played a very important part of the Downs life and was all due to the vision and goodwill of voluntary staff.

Our 1962 intake had 48 new people and, as already mentioned, by the end of the first week about 10 had dropped out. By the end of the year we were down to 24. I think there were about 9 of us who went on to the West Coast and a similar number who went to Ashley, with some staying on at Golden Downs. All of whom 'passed out' at the end of 1964.

We had a weekly syllabus where we were grouped into various forest operations such as thinning, pruning, releasing, and logging. Sometimes we might be on a particular operation for anything from a week to a month. We had very knowledgeable instructors, good with us and quite amazingly tolerant. Always disciplined and usually considerate. Most of our instructors (Digger, Ivan, Warren and Don), came from a background of general forestry, some such as Bud were ex Deer Cullers. Some had been Woodsman before us. Some like Warren had come from the army, (Ghurka), and some from Forestry in the UK. We had quite a range of personnel bringing a wide variety of skills. Periodically we would also be assigned to fire duties with Bob, then onto tool maintenance with Buster, who was a distant relative of mine. We also got some instruction on shooting.

We were paid £12 pound, 2 shillings and 6 pennies each fortnight. £5 pounds ($10) went straight to the cookhouse, leaving us with £7.2.6, ($14.50) and from this amount we had to keep ourselves in clothes, boots and socks. We were also able to buy firearms and ammunition. I was now 16 and bought from Don (one of our instructors), a cut down .303 which was in very good condition and a good shooter. A couple of times one of our instructors took us to the Gordons Creek rifle range and ran us through the 'sighting-in' process and gave us basic shooting instruction. Warren was an ex-army captain and had lots to offer us very raw and sometimes very useless pupils. By the end of our first range experience up at Gordons Creek (which we all loved), we were able to shoot with a good understanding of safety and a little bit of accuracy. I remember the first day so well, at the end of it we all had a huge 'bomb up' on the many big rocks 300 or 400 yards up the side of Wai-iti Ridge. Most of us had never shot at long distance and had certainly never seen the big spurts of dust fly when rocks were hit with heavy bullets. It was 'loose shooting' but great fun. We gradually became more aware of how to safely use our rifles and approach shooting. Sergeant Oxnam from the Wakefield Police came to the Downs and gave us our official Firearms Instruction and registered our rifles, the cost was five shillings (or 50 cents).

In the mornings before going to work we used to go over to the workshops and run up (start), the fire engines and drive them around the workshops. This was allowed and I guess we were just setting ourselves up to drive bigger trucks later. Personally I always enjoy driving the old quads which were ex Bren Gun carriers, V8 powered, with crash gearboxes. It took a lot of skill to drive these machines properly. One needed a good understanding of how to 'marry up' the revs with any particular selected gear. We all got plenty of instruction on fire control and firefighting practices and survival. This has stood all of us in good stead for our whole lives.

We did lots of 'thinning to waste' of Laricio Pine, it was quite soft cutting and gave us good practice at scarfing and direction felling, axe thinning and cross cutting. We had a few felling incidents; in our first year one of our intake, David G. who was a very popular boy, was killed in a logging accident. It was a brutal reminder to us all of the seriousness of our work when we were so young. Another of our intake, Lee, who was a keen caver, fell while deep underground in a cave on Mount Owen. This accident left Lee paralysed from the waist down, he was never able to work again and he has had a very difficult life. His only mobility is by wheelchair or driving a specialised vehicle.

Life was good at the Downs, but it was all hard work, and planting in the winter time in Nelson was really hard work. The ground was very stony and for a large portion of the time was nearly always frozen. I didn't like planting all that much so I turned myself into a really good poler. This was setting out the planting lines by placing Manuka poles into the ground to mark a line which the planter could follow. We use the 3-4-5 method of getting right angles, and compasses to get perfectly parallel lines. In those days we planted by parallel lines or the herringbone method, so polling perfect parallel lines across a steep stony hillside was far from easy. I well remember that I once got way ahead and had a weeks work done ahead of time. Then it rained and the ground thawed and nearly all of my poles fell down and had to be done again. I was gutted.

For a short period of three weeks I got sent into Nelson to work on the wharf, doing timber inspections for any possible bugs prior to the logs being exported. It was a very token presence. In fact it was just a formality and I had it extremely easy. Working on the wharf I very quickly got to know about union labour and the smuggling of transistor radios. Because I knew Ross C, I soon met his brothers, Max and Arthur C., both quite famous ex Deer Cullers who were working on the Nelson wharf. I came home with a new 'National Nine' transistor radio, as yet unheard of in the retail market in New Zealand. In fact they were unheard of here for many years, so it was obvious that the few that were here were smuggled.

From time to time Woodsmen were posted out to various places for work experience, and I was sent to Karamea for timber appraisals with O/C Ron

C. This was a neat place to work and I got to meet up with my relatives Uncle Frank and Auntie Shirley H., and their family, who lived by dairy farming in the district. Going to Karamea and meeting extended family formed the start of a lifelong friendship with my cousin Laura and her future family.

It was here at Karamea that I heard my first deer roar. We were working in the head of the Oparara River timber cruising, and we often went shooting deer at night with a spotlight. I also did my first beach surf casting and caught some big snapper fishing off the beach. Even though all our time at Karamea was baching, the very best food was never a problem. I remember the night we arrived in Karamea. We were dropped off at the Forestry bach, tea was already cooked for us. The Woodsman in charge said, “I will take you uptown and show you the bright lights”. It was still late night shopping on Fridays at that time. In Karamea there was a pub, a post office, a garage, and a shop. As we walked along the street a lady came out of the Post Office, calling out to me saying, “There is a telegram here for you”. I had only been in town for about half an hour but she was quite correct, there was one for me. How was that for small town stuff? It was from Rod Q., who was telling me that he was off to Westport. Another amazing detail I noticed at Karamea was that almost everyone in the district went to the pictures at Market Cross each Saturday night, regardless of what film might be showing. Everyone dressed up for the occasion in their Sunday best, so when Woodsmen turned up in shorts, jandals and a bush shirt hanging out Woodsman style, we quickly got the message that we needed to dress to a better standard. Now this wasn't so easy, mostly because we didn't have flash clothes, or at least not with us.

Later that year I went to Westport to work on Cruising under District Ranger, Bryan C. and Forest Ranger, Charlie B. in Pensini Creek, near the New River on the Buller. This was also another neat experience as, apart from work, in the evenings we regularly shot deer on the river flats. We once caught a grey Kiwi which is a huge bird. We kept it in the cupboard

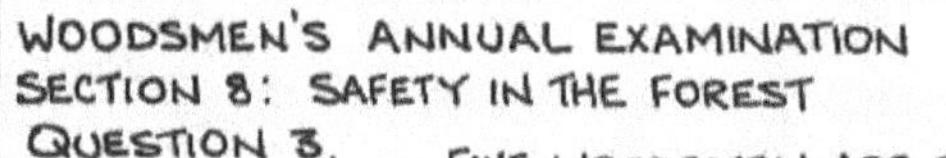

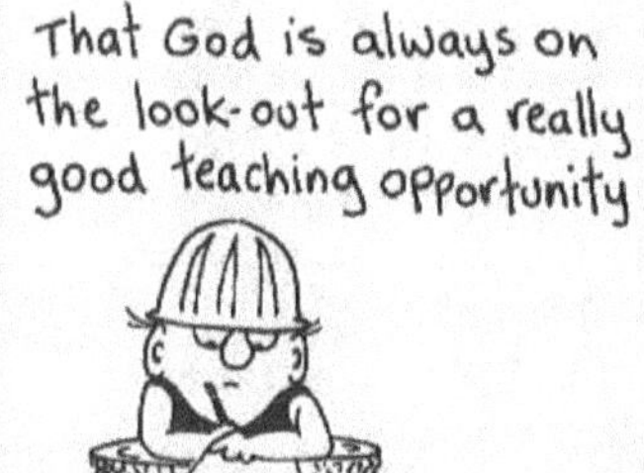

for a few days and fed it on worms while we got a camera sent up on the Newman's bus from Westport, so that we could take some photos of it.

Sometimes in the evenings, for fun at night, we shot eels in the Buller River after baiting them with old venison bones. None of these simple pastimes would occur too often in today's PC climate. We travelled back to Westport each Friday night and boarded with Mrs M. at her Palmerston Street home. We were staying with her the morning that President Kennedy was assassinated.

Back at Golden Downs, apart from the work and shooting, we all had girlfriends and went to many dances. We had, or borrowed motorbikes to travel around on, great in the summertime but nothing short of hellish in the winter when it was freezing. Sometimes in the winter we would be so cold we couldn't get out of the heavy bike gear for a half hour after arriving back. This was often not a happy situation when one was busting for a leak. We went into Nelson every second Friday night after payday, travelling on the Tapawera bus, which was run by Wadsworth's of Tapawera. We would eat in town (nearly always fish and chips), do the shopping for essentials, like bullets and boots, then go to the pictures. Quite often we would have a rifle with us, after getting it repaired or something. No problems in those days, one just carried it on the shoulder around the street. Not one person even blinked, when it was picture time we gave the rifle to the girl attendant at the pictures and then picked it up on the way out. The bus would leave as soon as the pictures were finished, but sometimes not everyone came back to camp, they would be shacked up with a new girlfriend. It was over an hours drive back to Golden Downs.

Sometimes we would start walking to our hunting blocks at midnight to arrive on the tops by 4 am when it was getting light. As 16 and 17 year olds, we were really super fit and we had become super keen in those days.

For my first Easter at the Downs I went back home, flying from Nelson to Dunedin on a South Pacific Airlines DC3. There was no pressurisation in those planes and my ears used to hurt like hell. They were very basic planes in those days, and as it was a very short time frame for a weekend, travelling from Nelson to Dunedin by air was the only real option. Otherwise it was two days travel by bus one way, and not feasible to travel so far in such a limited time. We never ever considered taking annual leave for such a trip, leave was saved for deerstalking trips. The cost of a return trip to Dunedin was only £5 (pounds), which equates to $10 today.

Intake mate Rod Q. and myself arranged to go hunting on Mount Owen during Queen's Birthday weekend. In the early 60's, Mount Owen was a fabled stalking place, with hundreds of deer which were always being talked about by all the older shooters. We got dropped off by a vehicle at the Dart River and then walked most of the day getting up onto the tops via the Rolling River and Billy's Spur. There was no real track, nearly all the shooting was done from the Owen River side of the mountain. The fact that we knew absolutely nothing wasn't even a faint deterrent. To give some idea and explanation of how little we knew in our planning, we thought we would need three meals a day, so we carried up to the tops (over 5000 feet), 12 tins of bully beef along with our other gear like sleeping bags and Primus etc. All for a two day trip. We never ate any of it.

We were about 2/3 of the way up Billy's Spur when we came across 2 hinds sleeping in the sun. We were so inexperienced that we never saw them until they jumped up, some 40 yards away. I guessed later that we would have been in full view of them for 50 yards or more before they finally spooked, at which point we couldn't fail to miss seeing them. They were so close we just looked along our barrels, never taking any real sighting, and we just fired away until they both dropped. That was the worst possible thing that could have happened, shooting by that shotgunning process and still getting them because, from then on, we felt we didn't need to carefully sight at anything, and in fact we had learned much less than nothing. We would have become better shots sooner if we had missed them completely. We took it all for granted. It was on the return from this trip that we found dozens of spawning trout in the creek near the head of the Rolling River. We shot seven deer for the weekend and arrived back at Golden Downs thinking we were already 'Shooters', having been up there and done it. But really, we were very much still only boys and only just beginning to learn a few things about everything, we

had a long way to go. But that taste was only a forerunner for many things to come. I shot a few deer and pigs in the Downs, but the open mountain tops, with the big numbers of deer, were a constant draw for me. I have never stopped thinking about how and when to get back there. I also used to shoot most weekends, up on the Wai-iti tops and Gordons Knob. All of us were so fit then and we could almost run non-stop up to the tops. Any of us could get to the top of Gordon's Knob, which was over 5000 feet, in an hour and a half. When I travel to Nelson now, I always look across at Gordons Knob and wonder how we ever ran up there? It would take me all day now and I would probably be sore for days afterwards. In fact in those days Gordon's Knob was a very open tussock, snowgrass type of open mountain. By mid 2015 it was almost totally regenerated scrub and would now be quite difficult to push through. We used to mostly get a deer each time we went out, additionally we shot many goats. None of us had vehicles and we walked non-stop on some Saturdays for up to 18 hours. Sundays were often very lazy days as we recovered from the Saturday's excursions. Talk about being keen, we could walk or run anywhere. We shot lots but we used to miss lots as well, when we should, or could have been getting them all. In those early years if we missed some deer, it didn't really worry us too much, we just carried on to the next spur or gully and found some more to shoot at.

Midway through 1963 I had a left-hand stock made for my rifle. It cost me £5 and it really made this into a completely different rifle to shoot. It was a very modern style for the day, having a rollover high comb cheek rest with a very comfortable pistol grip. This stock really 'made' the rifle and a few years later this alteration became quite a common change made by many other .303 owners. As mentioned, this very flash walnut stock cost me 5 pounds, or $10 in today's terms. If it were to be made today it would cost in the region of $1000. Today one cannot buy a dozen eggs for $10, so on that example, maybe in another 60 years a dozen eggs might cost nearly $1000, scary shit that is. The stock was made by Shale S., a talented Policeman from Nelson who created very fancy, high comb Monte Carlo / paddleboard styled stocks. While very stylish, it was a little on the heavy side, so over the years I gradually whittled off the rollover section which made it into a particularly nice stock and I still have it, even though it has been on about 10 different rifles.

As 16 or 17 year-old youths, Woodsmen were not allowed to have their rifle bolts during the week and we had to hand them into the Welfare Officer at the end of each weekend. On Friday night the draw for the weekend hunting blocks was posted on the bulletin board, and early every Saturday morning there was a mad rush to walk to ones block before daylight. A 10 mile hike before we started hunting was nothing to us then.

We were at Golden Downs to work and learn, if we had had our rifle bolts many of us would've been out hunting during the week nights, and would probably have been too tired to work properly, so it was a very sensible management philosophy. Small calibre rifles such as .22's were completely banned for Woodsmen, but there were some of us who had them hidden somewhere. Occasionally a few animals were shot during the week, not a lot, but it did happen. Hunting was banned during the week for all the best reasons, but we did sneak out when we were sure we could do it safely.

Many times, when the snow was down low, we were out hunting along the bush edges, looking for easy deer, but spotlighting was almost never done. Everyone carried home their pork or venison for the weekly dog food, so there was much beautiful fat pork fed to the dogs of that era. When we used to have wild pork from South Otago somehow it always seemed quite strong, whereas pork from Nelson was all always very mild and lovely to eat. I used to go hunting with borrowed dogs sometimes but much preferred to hunt around the mid slopes by myself. This was generally successful. I never owned hunting dogs at the Downs, so I only had to carry home the best cuts of meat for myself or to give to some village person. This was always a particularly good move, as they would generally invite you to dinner sometime, and while eating in the cookhouse was okay, home-cooked meals were something we all missed greatly.

In our second year we were allowed to live in the single men's huts. Each hut was 10' x 8' and had a small cast-iron potbelly stove, so we were able to cook some of our meat or fish, I can tell you that anything was a welcome change from cookhouse mass produced meals.

Over the years there were many interesting situations that happened regularly, and some of them almost daily. On one occasion, one of our crew, Morrie H. decided to go to Westport to buy an Ariel Square 4 motorbike. My part was to go with him and bring his old bike back. We hooned (sped), down to Westport in record time and caught up with Basil C., an ex Woodsman, to look at the new bike. For some reason the bike sale wasn't done, so Morrie and I rode all around Westport and the local beaches, and then late in the afternoon headed back to the Downs. Morrie's Triumph bike did not last the distance, in fact it broke down not far up the lower Buller Gorge. We shoved it in the bushes on the side of the road and started walking. From the Ohikanui we got a ride to Inangahua Junction, from there we walked almost to the Iron Bridge, where a mini car stopped to pick us up. Quite amazing, as it was nearly dark and even more amazing was that it was an ex Woodsman, Norm S. from the 1955 intake, who delivered us right back to the front hostel.

Golden Downs Woodsmen used to have an annual sports competition with Kaingaroa Woodsmen which included rugby. During a game, one of our boys was having a good dust up right near where I was standing on the sidelines. Quite naturally I was giving some verbal support, but not for long. Our Instructor (an ex Ghurka), gave me a good chop right in the solar plexus, which immediately shut up my yap.

One night a few of us noticed a huge red sky appear from the north east, it was very spectacular, and it was not long after that we were told it was caused from nuclear testing in the Pacific Ocean. I don't know whether that was true, but it certainly made for good conversation for awhile.

There were a number of driving incidents, everyone sort of fancied themselves as a good driver but actually, most were not. One night while coming home in the gang bus, a J3 Bedford, with Des T. driving down a long straight on Duff Road, nearly back to headquarters, Des decided to show us all how well he could change gears. Double clutching was a specialty and very necessary for some vehicle models. J3 Bedford gearboxes were all synchromesh except for low or first gear. Des smartly changed down from 3rd to 2nd, all of us in the back could see what was happening, then without further ado he changed to first, not an easy change but he married up the revs perfectly and slotted it in well. He would have been proud to have pulled it off. But then, because the truck was rolling so slowly down the slope, about walking speed, he jumped out and ran alongside for a few yards. He must have had it planned for some time but what he didn't know was that Jim C. the Officer in Charge of Golden Downs was driving behind us in his Vanguard Ute. Oops!

Another time with Davey M. at the wheel of an old gang truck, loaded with about 8 or 10 Woodies in the back, we were driving onto a newly prepared skidder site at Kings Ridge. I reckon it was 100 meters square and was flat as anything, completely clear except for one large rock right in the middle. This rock was about as big as a spare wheel and at least 18” high, Davey seemed to be heading straight for it. The truck canopy had a small window looking forward through the cab, about as big as a shoebox and all of us were trying to look through it. We all thought that Davey was ‘having us on’ and would soon swerve away but no, somehow he drove right over the top of it. Near impossible but it did happen, and there was lots of crunching.

One of our intake, Trevor G, was a great guy but not good on his feet, especially in the scrub. He could and did trip on anything, even as small as a single bracken stick. Poor old Trevor was always arsing up. He also had some family in the soap making business, accordingly he was nicknamed Soapy, but his nickname became legendary, as whenever he fell over, everyone would loudly call out “Soapy”! From then on, when anyone fell over or arsed up everyone would call “Soapy”, and that name continued for many years.

During the Golden Downs stint (which was for me a 2 year period), I was sent up the Wangapeka River on a track cutting mission. Andy A. was a 2nd year Woodsman and our party leader. Andy, Rod and I were the very first Woodsmen to go to the Wangapeka to work. Our boss was Ross C. The job was a sort of additional periodic job and other Woodsmen followed us. We learned how to set up a Deer Culler type camp, with a big heavy tent and galley sides, with a huge fly. We regularly shot good numbers of deer after work. We loved it all except for the wasps. They were so bad that when eating your lunch at midday, one had to keep moving, otherwise they would land on your lunch and start eating too, these wasps were protein hungry. Many times I would get my lunch ready then head off up the track eating it as I went. This Wangapeka track work was a great experience and as we got to go shooting every night after work, it was just heaven for me. Being so fit, sometimes I would climb up Mount Patriarch after work and shoot a few deer, then climb back down in the dark. Nelson district did not produce heads of any decent size but it had lots of deer so we all got heaps of experience. All the Nelson tops had a huge advantage of not having any 'monkey scrub'.* One could climb through the beech forest and get straight out onto the open tops. I was to learn much more about monkey scrub later when I transferred to the West Coast.

It was quite possible to look along some of the better river flats and see mobs of a dozen or more deer grazing in the evening, a good shooter could rack up some good tallies, but we were still only getting one or two at a time. I remember one particular evening where I spotted 12 deer grazing on a set of grassy terraces in the Wangapeka River not too far above the Rolling River confluence. I was positioned approximately 100 feet above them. The maximum distance I had to shoot was not over about 200 yards. A good shooter would have cleaned up the lot. When I fired my first shot, which missed, they all ran closer towards me, and as I fired some more they kept running closer. It seemed like the gunshot sound was bouncing off the terraces behind them and scared them towards me. To this day about 60 years later, I am completely appalled that my shooting was so poor (I used a whole 10 shot magazine), that I didn't knock one of them over, despite being in a perfect shooting position. And it was getting better by the second as the animals came closer. I sometimes still try to analyse what happened there. I have always felt it wasn't just a case of 'buck fever'. While sometimes I have had that feeling, but never for long and never at the shooting stage, I quite honestly think that in my total inexperience, I must have been resting my barrel on a rock or hard surface. At that time I hadn't learned or had a single clue about 'barrel harmonics' and it was not until many years later that I acquired some knowledge about that. If that was the case then all my shots would have likely landed at least a couple of feet high.

We did get lots of experience setting up camps and tents in the typical Deer Culler style. The track cutting was also interesting. We worked in all weathers, cutting trees, digging benches, blasting rocks, making water tables etc, under the guidance of leading hand, Ross C. Ross went on to write a number of books called the 'Murphy Series', although despite having known him well and liked him, and hunted under his instruction, I did not really get to grips with his stories. I also did get to shoot alongside his two brothers in the Wangapeka. Arthur and Max C. were wonderful shots and were Deer Culler legends. I was always impressed by their skills and their books. One night Rod and I arrived at Kiwi Hut after midnight, having walked in from the Dart, and they, Max and Arthur, were already there. They fed us some of their favourite hot curry which was so hot I had to go down to the river at midnight and bathe my head and drink cold water. That put me off hot curry forever.

Over the next year or so, Rod and I used to go back to the Wangapeka shooting at every chance we could get. We used to get dropped off at the Dart River and walk from there. We were always cadging a ride somewhere. There were no flash torches in those days but we did see lots of glow worms. We used to sleep under a huge rock camp in the lower Rolling, or in the camps we had built earlier. These camps were built in the old Deer Culler style with sleeping quarters and a galley, all covered with a heavy fly.

One night while sleeping in one of these camps at Appletree Flat, just below King's Hut, I recall a possum woke us by noisily scrounging around in our galley, and I decided to shoot it. At the time we were using our rifles and boots for pillows so I dragged my rifle out to do the job. The possum scarpered before I was ready to shoot and that was the end of that. We were well awake, so I decided to read by candlelight for a while. Soon I dropped back off to sleep and the candle somehow tipped over and set alight all the bracken fern we had been sleeping on. Why I awoke later I do not know, but there was a patch of embers about 2 ft square and possibly a foot deep burning between us. It wasn't a real problem beating it out, but in the bully beef tin, which was being used for a candlestick holder, I had previously placed a half dozen .303 bullets that I had taken out of my pockets before going to sleep (in our clothes). By sheer luck we managed to get it sorted before the rounds had 'cooked off'. The outcome from that little effort was a huge never to be forgotten lesson. The fore-end had burned completely off Rod's jungle carbine rifle.

All the creeks around the Wangapeka region held lots of Blue Ducks, but usually we would hear them before we saw them. One afternoon while climbing around the southern end of Mount Patriarch, not too far below the top, I found a rock chimney, and rather adventurously decided to climb up it. It wasn't too long before I had my feet on one side and my back to the other. I was able to support myself and work my way up, but near the top it got very scary, and the choice to go back down was not really an option. The situation may well have turned out very badly as I had no idea of what was on top, or whether I could even exit the top, or whatever? I might be able to climb down the other side? I certainly had no experience in rock climbing, but I managed to keep my nerve and carefully keep going up. I cannot remember how far it was, maybe only 60 to 100 feet but I do remember that I was so 'whacked' when I finally got to the top, which was about 10 feet across, that I lay down and didn't move for at least half an hour. Once I was well rested I sat up and saw, away over on a rocky slip, 2 deer. One of them was standing with its head directly behind the other one's chest so I took careful aim and shot both of them with one shot. The walk down the western side wasn't too hard, definitely easier than the way up. I just love shooting in those beautiful areas of Beech Forest where the bush line opens directly onto the snow grass.

When I was transferred to Karamea and Westport I shot a number of deer around the bush flats by stalking at last light or spotlighting, it was great fun and very good practice.

We travelled from Golden Downs by Newman's buses to Westport. The upper Buller Gorge was sort of regarded as a fearsome road in those days, no part of the Dublins Terrace was yet sealed, it was a very lumpy, wavy sort of road. My first trip down there was the day the Lyell pub burned down. It was still smoking when we went past. Today we travel down in our cars and do the trip from the Hope to the Iron Bridge in under an hour, back then it used to be about four hours. The road was upgraded to a first class highway soon after the 1968 Inangahua earthquake.

At the end of our first two years, we were all offered a choice; either a posting to Ashley Forest in Canterbury, to Totara flat on the West Coast or to just stay on at the Downs. I chose to go to the Coast, a decision I have never regretted, and so started many more fabulous years, which I will always rank as some of the best times of my life. Coming from quite a religious family I was never a drinker at the Downs but on shifting to the West Coast it wasn't too long before I set about catching up on that.

Before long and because of my previous experience and ability at Timber Cruising, I was promoted to Cruising Officer status and placed on the books as such, a position normally reserved for at least Forest Foreman or Ranger level. All this while I was only 18 years old and still a junior Woodsman!

Another legend that started off in our time, there was a Forrester called Ross W. who went to work every day. That is, 7 days a week with no days off. Anyone who was out bush on weekends regularly saw Ross or his forestry vehicle somewhere around the hills, he would be out doing his sample plots or whatever he was up to. Also at that time, our cookhouse used to always have luncheon roll in every one of the sandwiches every day, and so those sandwiches became known as 'Ross sandwiches'.

I continued in the Forestry for over 46 years, made up of 11 years on the Coast and the rest at Whangapoua forest on the Coromandel. I retired from Forestry at age 61 to go commercial fishing. My time since 2007 is spent about 60/40 between the West Coast and the Coromandel. I still loosely keep in contact with Terry J, John L. and Rod Q. from my own intake and also Ian L. (1955), Cam B. (1957), Mike M. (1964), Andy M, ex District Ranger and Peter H. ex Conservator of Forests, Auckland, who in turn keep in touch with some of the other guys. To a large extent we still have quite an intake group and general forestry network, which has become very special in the past few years. I have redeveloped and reproduced several New Zealand Forest Service emblems in sticker form and I pass them on to others at our reunions. New Zealand Forest Service finished in 1987, which is now over 38 years ago. The Woodsman School finished up about 1983 which is now over 42 years ago. Who would have thought that since the end of the Woodsman scheme, there have been four major, full scale, well attended Golden Downs reunions, and there is still a strong loyalty amongst former members that will not likely be seen again. Yep, the New Zealand Forest Service Woodsman Training Schools were a huge success and probably much greater than the founders ever first envisaged. Woodsmen from all the schools, Golden Downs, Kaingaroa, Aupouri, Ashley, Dusky, Totara Flat and Berwick contributed proudly, from hands-on work to senior management in the forest industry and other business paths as well. A life that we were all very fortunate to have been part of.

* *Monkey Scrub is a mix of Turpentine and Olearia type species, a tangled mess of usually very dense, tight growth, almost impossible to get through unless a track is cut. It grows to nearly head height. It's a level of sub alpine scrub between the upper bush line and the snow grass, and only grows above podocarp forests (Rimus etc). It can be seen on 'Google Earth' above the upper bush level, mostly in Westland. It's put many a hunter off going up to the tops.*

## Terry's Tales.

During our Woodsman training one of our jobs was upgrading of the Wangapeka Track. We went in groups of 4 at a time and we were dropped off at Tadmor where we were met by Ranger Ross C. He took us out to his house where his good wife gave us a lovely morning tea and goodies before we climbed aboard the forestry Commer flat-deck runabout and headed across the Rolling River.

As it happened, there had been a bit of rain and the Rolling was carrying a fair amount of extra water. It looked okay but the vehicle kept leaving the bottom and was heading downstream towards the rapids. I remember there were thoughts among us on the deck that maybe we should 'abandon ship'. Anyway, we did get through okay and continued up the Wangapeka river until we arrived at the base camp at Apple-tree Flat, which was to be our home for the next week. I was lucky enough to do two stints on the track, most of the work was cutting / benching. I can't remember exactly who was on each trip, but there was usually a 2nd year Woodsman with us to act as a supervisor, having had that extra years experience. Ross C. did pop in to see how we were going occasionally. John B. (Baldy), was definitely with us on the 2 week stint because the two of us went deer stalking up the Grassy Slip, and on the way down in the dull twilight we almost stepped over a bluff to the river way down below. Baldy had shot a deer and we decided to get out before it got dark. The deer had actually crashed over a bluff when he shot it and it landed in the forks of a Beech tree. I kept a photo of that for years.

Bill P. from Dunedin (a really good 'feather-weight' wrestler), was on one of the trips. A funny incident happened on this trip involving Bill. Being an open type tent fly camp the possums tended to sneak in and they could get into our tucker supplies that were generally stacked around or near the open fire where we did our cooking. Most nights we would be awakened in the early hours by the sniffling noises of a possum going through our supplies. Of course they would get a short shift, but early one morning there was a startled yell and scream from Bill and here's this possum perched on Bill's chest (on top of his sleeping bag), peering into his face. Needless to say, all hell broke loose. The possum flew out the door with four of us after it, and it escaped up the apple tree beside our tent base. It was perched a little high for us to reach with a slasher so it was suggested I grab my 303. I managed to figure out that my (open) sights were on the silhouette of the Jacko* (all of 7 or 8 feet away), anyway, boom, and something fell down the side of the canvas and the possum took off across the flat. We left it till morning to see where it had stopped running. My reputation as a marksman was on the line. In the daylight we found the Jacko, completely gutted and it was the guts that had slid down the canvas. That one didn't pinch our tucker again.

One day Ross arrived and walked us up the track to the Branch (I think it was called), at the base of the Lunar Saddle looking down into the Lunar Basin, and of course, the track then continues on to Karamea. We spent a night or two in the hut while Ross headed back home. These were really good trips out in the hills and will always be very memorable.

** A 'Jacko' is a slang term for an opossum.*

**Peter Christie.** The Bloke from Gore who rolls his R's.

My name is Peter, I arrived at Golden Downs when I was 15 years and 3 months old following a two-day trip from Gore, it wasn't long before I started to wonder what I'd walked into. There were lots of bullshit initiation ceremonies but as many of us had been through that sort of bloody nonsense at high school we quickly banded together into groups, and when groups of the second-year guys arrived in the middle of the night to bully us they met some pretty stiff resistance. So the bullying knocked off pretty quickly. But it was a real education, we soon realised that the more we stuck together the better we were.

My first job at Golden Downs was thinning Douglas Fir which had been planted some 20 to 30 years earlier at the standard spacing of 6 feet x 6 feet. We were using axes and 3 foot long crosscut saws. Of course, as most of us were fresh from school, our hands were very soft, we all had blisters by the mile. The advice we were given was, 'piss on your hands, it'll toughen them up'. Initially that made them sting like crazy, but eventually the pain went away. It did make it a bit tough eating ones lunch with 'pissed on' hands. We did this thinning for about three months, interspersed with days filled with learning about various tools and how to use them, which was most often constructing firebreaks.

Our favourite boozer was the Korere Valley hotel. We could book in on Friday night, two or three rooms, and if we topped and tailed we could sleep up to 10 or 12 guys for a night, for $2. During the day we would often go and help the raspberry picking girls pick raspberries, and then of course they would come to the hotel and help us party. We often used the Korere Valley straight as a speedway test run for our motorbikes and old bombs of cars. We measured out a one mile length of straight road in front of the pub. The fastest run anyone ever got was 112 miles per hour by Greg G., on a big BSA Goldflash motorbike. He went on to become a traffic cop after Woodie graduation.

Our Welfare Officer at Golden Downs was a man called Len C. Len was physically one of the most impressive people that I've ever met in my life. He stood about 5 foot eight tall and probably weighed about 22 stone and it was all bone and bloody muscle. He started a wrestling club at the Downs and we competed in amateur bouts in Nelson. He had a great understanding of the psychology of young boys, especially of us as teenagers. Sometimes, when he realised that a few of us were getting pissed off with the whole system and were ready to rebel, he would walk into the lounge at night and say "If any of you jokers have got a chip on your shoulder and if you want to take it out on somebody, take it out on me". He would be standing in the middle of the lounge and he would encourage us to attack him. Then, anything from 10 to 20 boys would just jump him and he would disappear under a pile of bodies, a real scrum. Next thing there would be a scream from the middle of the mass, no one knew what was going on and / or if anyone was getting really damaged. Boys would be going in all directions, Len would've been on the bottom of the pile and would have bitten someone's finger or ear or something else, whatever he could sink his teeth into. It was rough but it relieved a lot of stress, and was great fun. Always lots of laughs afterwards. One night in the lounge he showed us his scrapbook. During the war he had been in the Merchant Navy, and every time they were coming in to port, sailors on the ship would radio ahead and organise a wrestling bout. Len's fight diary had about three hundred fights in it, with only a handful of defeats. He was a great man and a wonderful Welfare Officer for us.

In the winter of 1956, we worked in the nursery at Tapawera. This was a make or break job for some of our intake. It was freezing cold, your fingers just about froze off, there was no reprieve for the whole day. The rows of pine seedlings had already been wrenched (tap roots cut below ground level), and we had to then remove them from the ground, carry them to tables where they were sorted into bundles of 25, then tied with thin strips of flax. The roots were trimmed to a uniform length and then dipped in a fairly thick slurry of water, clay, soil, sawdust and manure before being potted into bags prior to being transported to the planting areas. Our hands froze, they were wet and covered in mud slurry all day. Our fingers and knuckles cracked with the cold and there was no letup. Few of us had gloves and we couldn't have afforded them anyway, even if they had been available. A lot of us started smoking at this time because the warmth a tiny cigarette could generate felt wonderful. We all reckoned if we could survive that first winter in the nursery we could survive and put up with anything and of course most of us did.

At one time there was a lot of bad feeling within the 1956 intake. In our 4th year we were supposed to be being trained to be used in Leading Hand or Foremen roles, supervising the new intakes, and being trained in more specialised jobs, but we ended up just planting alongside the Reg 130 workers (guys on contract, paid by every 100 trees they planted). We were on wages and sometimes planting two to three times more per day, but for less money. At other times we were planting in places like Long Gully, where the conditions were so bad we had to carry bags of dirt so as to be able to plant trees in the rocky ground. So we were constantly harassed for not planting as much as other teams around the forest.

We started a soccer team at Golden Downs about 1957 and we we did reasonably well in that first year. When we came back in 58 we had three great coaches who were also our forestry instructors, they were determined to make things go well. One of them was Peter E., an Englishman. Bruce H. was a Scot, Davy M. was Welsh and Kevin D. was a Geordie. Under their coaching we won the Nelson Junior championship in 1959, plus the Gould & Tout Knockout Cup. Many of us got to play for the senior teams if they happened to be a player or two short. As Goalie, I was always very proud of having the best figures in one season.

We were allowed firearms at the Downs but we had to hand the bolts in on a Sunday night and get them back the following Friday for the weekend. Often we would shoot a deer or pig and Greasy Jim, the cook would give us extra in the meals for it. His wife looked like the Wicked

Witch of the West, one time there was uproar in the dining room when her wig dropped into the soup. They weren't very well liked and their cooking was less than good. They were eventually replaced by Don and Mary T., who were vastly better.

We often went into Nelson, for dances or sporting events, or maybe just a party on the beach. Often there were stray dogs on the beach or wandering the streets, and many of us kept a few dog collars handy to grab a hold of these pooches. If they looked Ok we'd take them back to the Downs and try them out as pig dogs. Some worked really well, some not so much and they ended up staying on the hill. There was a Constable at Wakefield who reckoned we were mostly doing a good public service getting these strays off the street. Sometimes however, we picked up the wrong dog and the owners would ring the police and say, "we've lost a dog". Constable B at Wakefield would say, "Hmmm, there was a bunch of Woodsmen playing rugby in Nelson today, I wonder"? One of the lads once nabbed a large Red Setter dog. Apparently, it was worth thousands. The Constable came out, checked the cages, retrieved the dog and never said a word to us about it.

Our OC, Jim C, came looking for some volunteers to give him a hand for a bit of community work in the Tapawera area. Half a dozen of us were up for it, and on Saturday morning off we went. We had a good day doing all sorts of jobs, but were absolutely buggered at the end of the day. On our way home, Jim pulled into the Pub at the Kohatu Junction and said "Come on boys you've done a bloody great job I'll shout you a beer or two". We all said, "Sorry Jim, that ain't gonna happen. Old Ma Grindle, she won't let us in the door". Ma never let any Woodsman into her pub. Jim said, "Nah, we're going in", and she yelled at him that he should know better than to bring Woodsman into her establishment. Jim never batted an eyelid, he told her that his boys had been working for old people all day around the district and they deserved a beer. She just yelled louder, told us to get out. By now the boss was getting very angry and he gave her an ultimatum; "Either these boys get a beer or I'll blacklist you in Golden Downs. No Forestry personnel will ever come here again". After a bit more bluster, she backed down and we got our beer.

We had an instructor named Jack B. Jack was a paratrooper during the Second World War, who had parachuted into Arnhem. He used to drive us around in a 7 ton Bedford flat nose truck. It would take about 25 to 30 boys, it had a canvas canopy on the back end and that was how we used to go to work and come home. Up in long gully one night, just after 4 pm, we're about a mile down the road going home and Jack miscalculated the corner and next thing we are on a 45° angle leaning up against a stand of Douglas Fir trees and the only thing holding the truck up was the fact that the canopy had been well built. Jack was a lovely man, he stood there and said in his very broad Yorkshire accent, "Fookin ell, I got dat wrong dint eye". Then he said that if we got the truck back on it's feet he'd get us back to the cookhouse in time for dinner. We said, "No thanks Jack". We all started walking and took a shortcut, straight across the river. The next day the Beddy had been checked over during the night, the mechanical staff said "She's alright, she's good to go, no damage done". Jack said, "Right-o boys, on the truck". We all just stood there, nobody moved. "Move" said Jack, "You've gotta go to work". Nobody moved, and then a voice piped up, "We'll go to work but you're not driving", so it was a big discussion between the Woodsman School and the Woodie gang. They eventually found another driver. So from then on Jack never drove us anywhere. We continued to work with Jack, he eventually moved down to Totara Flat on the West Coast. We never again were in a truck that Jack was driving, at Golden Downs, anyway.

The food at the cookhouse was often less than growing, hard working young men needed (or thought they needed). I was always hungry, most of us usually asked the cooks for seconds every evening. We began supplementing the evening meal with cookies that we could buy from the canteen, and then we discovered Rusks. It quickly got to the point where the canteen sold out of rusks and they had to double, then triple and then quadruple their weekly order. One night several mums from the village came knocking on our Woodie doors asking if they could buy some of the rusks back from us for their kids, we had bought out every rusk in the shop.

Quite few of us were keen fishermen, and we didn't mind bending the rules. There was a big 'do' coming up and the cook wanted to feed about 100 people something special. So we flogged a roll of rabbit netting from the workshops and stretched it across a piece of the Motupiko river where the water was only waist deep. With about a dozen lads we walked several hundred yards of the river, beating the water with sticks and we ended up with enough trout for Don and Mary to feed the whole lot.

We did about a 2 - 3000 acre burn off. It was on the border of Golden Downs and the Tasman Forest. We worked on it for quite a few weeks. It was mainly all bracken fern with logs and cutover slash. Once the fire was lit, lots of birds and animals such as possums, rabbits, etc., were trying to escape the flames and they were running in every direction. Many burning animals escaped across the firebreak boundaries into the Tasman Forest.

We were trying to intercept them but we didn't have a hope, the burning animals started multiple fires across the road, which we then had to fight. Tasman lost about 25 acres of standing trees that day.

One of our jobs was seed collecting, we spent time at many sites around Nelson. Climbing Nigra (Pinus Laricio) at about 60 to 70 feet to get the cones from the top of the tree was relatively easy. Strap a canvas planting bag around your waist and up you went. Most of the good cones were right at the top, we soon discovered that the trees were strong enough to hold us, even if we got adventurous. On the Wadsworth homestead at Tapawera, there was a line of huge Douglas Fir trees (100 feet plus), lining the sides of a very steep gully. After realising that it was a bloody long way up and back down, some enterprising chap worked out that it was much easier to cross directly to the next tree if your bag wasn't full yet. If one started the tree swaying, with a bit of effort rocking back and forwards, one could safely cross to the next tree while almost at the top. We had quite a few close calls but no serious injuries. It was lots of fun until one of our guys fell, breaking collar bone and leg. With the height of the trees plus the height of the gully we were overhanging, it was a long way down. When the cone bag was full, usually it was just dropped, with a loud yell of "TIMBER" to warn anyone below. No one ever owned up to dropping a bag of cones on one very unpopular instructor who just didn't hear the 'timber' call. His collar bone was broken, but his helmet did it's job in all other respects.

We collected seed from European and Japanese Larch on the western slopes of Spooners Range. These trees weren't tall, but the branches were very brittle and because we had so many 'near misses' it ended up that only the lightweights amongst us were able to climb. Even then it was a risky business, no room for horseplay here. Sometimes though, safety went overboard.

As part of the training at Dusky Forest, it was decided to send a crew of Woodies to Queenstown, to recover seed from some magnificent 100 + year old Douglas Firs between Queenstown and Glenorchy. The preparation for this expedition was something to see. We didn't just rock up, climb the trees, collect the cones and go home. Hell no. We were in the public eye, safety was paramount. The Otago Harbour board was approached and they supplied and erected big cargo nets using ropes and blocks and tackles, to string the nets between the trees. It took longer to erect the safety gear in the lower foliage than it did to collect the seed. What should've taken a couple of days lasted for many weeks.

One of our lads, foolhardy, or perhaps just adventurous (you could also read- braindead, thick, stupid), thought that a group of branches looked thick and strong enough to be like a slide. He started just fine but then about 3/4 of the way down he slipped through a gap in the branches he hadn't seen and finished with a broken leg, collarbone and a couple of ribs. He later reckoned it wasn't anything too serious.

I did my third year at Totara Flat with George J. as the Officer in Charge at Granville Forrest. I think we were sent down there primarily to make sure that they had plenty of labour to handle the nursery work. To live and work on the West Coast at that time required a certain dress standard, we weren't allowed to wear the garish, outlandish clothes that we wore in Nelson, especially at the dances. Proper attire was a suit, or sports jacket and grey trousers, which most of us didn't own. If we went to a dance, we couldn't ask a girl for a dance unless we had first asked her mum (for a dance). Dance with Mum, then ask Mum for permission to ask the daughter. Or, if you had impressed Mum, she might suggest that you asked the daughter.

We played Rugby in the Greymouth Junior competition on Saturdays and then on Sundays we often made up the numbers in the Reefton Seniors competition. Most of the guys in those teams were Bushman or Miners and they were 'hard bastards'. Mostly they weren't very fast but they knew every trick in the book, and a lot that weren't. We often got pounded. One of the referees was a Catholic Priest from Reefton, who ran a very tight game of rugby. If there was any nonsense on the field he would stop the game, bring out a couple of sets of boxing gloves and he and the offender would 'duke it out' on the side of the field. Once you'd learned a lesson, the game could continue. No more dirty tactics on the field after that. As I said, we got pounded.

Totara Flat was a cold place, each of our huts had a little stove in it but getting dry wood to burn was always a problem. However, the railway line ran right alongside the camp and almost every night a train with hundreds of wagons of coal would pull up and wait for a while, sometimes an hour or two. Being enterprising types we quickly learned to scale the wagons and just throw lumps of coal off onto the ground. Occasionally a railway guy, maybe a driver or some such, would run down the line screaming at

us. We just scarpered of course, and the railways guys didn't have the time, inclination or the means to throw the coal back up onto the wagons. After the train departed, or at first light, we came back with our sacks, buckets or wheelbarrows and picked up the lumps. Oh warm cosy huts.

Eventually I was a foreman at Rankleburn, and then because I was getting fed up with the whole system, I joined the Forest Biology Survey, working out of the Forest Research Institute. I did about two or three months there, mainly doing insect investigations and looking at anything weird going on with the various viruses that were problematic in the forests. I put in for a job with the Justice department and once I was told that I'd got the job, I moved up to Tūrangi, where I ran the Forestry operations for the Justice Department. At that time the Justice Department had a lot of land in forests and that was primarily to provide a work / rehabilitation opportunity for prisoners, youth offenders, etc. These forests existed all through New Zealand, from Southland to Northland.

## Butch.

Our intake was responsible for Woodies not being allowed vehicles. After the following event anyone who had a vehicle had to hide them in the scrub somewhere.

Labour weekend was approaching fast and beer was the preferred option for the weekend. So the Ford model A was fuelled up from (you can probably guess where), and off it went to Top House. We had a huge beer order from a lot of the boys. Those on board best remain anonymous. After

a few beers and on the way back, the old Ford, which only had a rag top which was down, approached the Gordons Creek bridge. She didn't quite make the corner and rolled over a small bank and landed with her feet in the air. One of the Woodies got caught under the car but wasn't hurt.

Somehow the word soon got back to the hostels and next minute there were Woodies everywhere. We thought that they came to help roll the car onto its feet, but no, they were all trying to grab what beer wasn't broken first! Getting the car off the guy was the second thing to happen. It's funny now but not so much at the time.

We had an older guy in our intake and he was quite a knowledgeable character. He was telling us how he could hot wire a vehicle. So, as we could no longer have vehicles, perhaps it would be appropriate if we used one of theirs? Saturday night came around, he hot wired the Bedford station wagon and off we went. Past the main office into town, got some beer and off we went to a couple of parties in Nelson. At some ungodly hour we headed home and parked the station wagon back in its slot.
Now when I returned as an instructor it always amazed me that no one ever cottoned on to the fact that the running book was way out and the truck's fuel gauge was nearly on empty. (The trucks had to be filled every Friday night in case of fire call outs). Perhaps they thought that Woodies commandeering a truck for the night wasn't too far out of reasonable behaviour? It happened four times I'm aware of and none got caught. It always amazed me that no one spotted it driving around Nelson it the middle of the night.

I can't remember why, but one of our intake decided to have a ride up the hose tower. He was hooked on to the power lift that pulled hoses up to the top. When he got quite high off the ground someone turned the switch off and he was left hanging there. The sandflies chewed the shit out of him as he had no shirt on, and it was a fair while before his 'mates' came back to let him down. How he had the strength to hang there for so long I have no idea. Silly bugger.

There used to be a stores cart come to the hostels once a week. One of our intake stole a lighter and the Dutchman who owned the cart said that if it wasn't returned he wasn't ever coming back. So OC. Cliff K., held a meeting and gave the offender a chance to come clean. When no one admitted the crime, Cliff said, "I'll leave it to you guys to sort out, otherwise the cart won't be back". A few of us were appointed to do a room search while the rest stayed in the lounge. The lighter and culprit were soon found and he was made to strip off and run the gauntlet. Two lengths of the hostel corridor while he was beaten with knotted towels. There was no more stealing.

We had a slightly backward chap in our intake. Another of our intake took him up to the dog kennels and supposedly attempted something sexual. The victim came screaming back to the hostel yelling "so and so tried to root me". A few of us waited for the alleged offender to turn up. When he saw us (about eight of us), he took off towards the village. We caught him at the tennis courts. There was a huge puddle near him and each time he tried to run away he was punched back into the puddle. He left that night never to be seen again.

We had a shortish guy in our intake. While waiting for the Friday night bus to take us back to the Downs a couple of Nelson chaps pushed and bumped past us to get into the fish and chip shop. Then one of them said "Bloody Woodsman shit" One of the 6 foot tall second year guys went to grab him and give him a clip, but our wee fella stepped up and said "I'll deal with him". The guy ripped the new shirt off our wee fella's back so then the wee fella hooked into him, knocking the mouthy one into the shop window. The shop owner rang the police who sent three cops. One driver, and the wee fella was stuck in between the two big cops in the back seat. His head hardly reached their shoulders. He was a great guy and we keep in touch but unfortunately he was sacked.

**Sally Quickfall.** *(nee Croawell)*

I have always thought of myself as a forestry brat, I was born and bred into it and then started my career in the NZ Forest Service, following in my father's footsteps. My Dad, Ralph Croawell joined the NZFS after returning from WWII, and after four and a half years in bombers, he was pleased to have an outdoors lifestyle. I was born in Havelock while he was OC of Rai Valley Forest, moving to Balmoral Forest when I was three. By the time I was turning 10, he was the OC at Golden Downs, so my formative years were spent growing up in the freedom of these isolated communities, providing a wonderful childhood and fostering in me my huge love for our land, and especially the more remote areas. A lifetime of heading into the hills has ensued.

I joined the Forest Service early in 1978 and my parents had high hopes for me becoming a Forester (working in the more professional side of the job), but after two years at University I knew I wanted a more practical career. Summer holiday jobs spent crunching numbers on computers made sure of that. Like all NZFS Trainees I spent my first year in a Forest doing all facets of work in the field, very similar to what the Woodsmen did in their first two years. I was sent to work amongst the gorse of Ashley Forest, and this was definitely the hardest year of my time in production forestry. Not helped by my Foreman's first words to me when getting on the gang bus that first day, "As far as I am concerned you have taken the seat that a good guy could have had". I'm not a stubborn person but that statement did not have the effect on me he wanted, whenever I felt like quitting I pondered those words and became more committed to sticking it out.

Physically it was a tough job for a lass straight out of school, but then it was for quite a few of the blokes also. That year was physically and mentally tough, but still I preferred it to the academic lifestyle. I returned to Ranger School after Uni and qualified as one of the Forest Service's first female Rangers. I loved the job. Looking back, mainly, I think it was a combination of the outdoor work with enough office stimulation to keep it interesting. The village lifestyles of which I was well versed in, having grown up in them, and the fantastic camaraderie that was to be had amongst the workers, whether Rangers, Woodsman, Labourers, Foresters and Office Admin staff. We worked hard and I have to say we played pretty hard too! It was a good life!

The four year Ranger School course involved three months a year in the classroom on block courses at Whakarewarewa in Rotorua, at the Forestry Training School. That was when we all came together and my memories of those times are some of the best of my life. We were young, free and had some money in our pockets, a heady combination in our late teens and early twenties. The courses themselves were pretty technical, we got a fantastic well rounded training in all things forestry related, extremely interesting and requiring us to knuckle down for quite a bit of the time, to ensure we passed our exams at the end. It was on the Environmental block course that I realised there was more to forestry than just timber production, and a strong desire to go into Recreational Forestry was born in me.

I was lucky to get an opportunity to be based on Stewart Island in my third year of training, and I knew then that the siren call of the hills was more alluring than producing good timber. As was the way with our training, we had to be experienced in all aspects, so on completion of my training I was transferred from Southland to the West Coast of the South Island, based at Kaniere Forest, running the silviculture gangs (gangs of labourers doing forestry work). I had about 40 guys all up, including a few contracting gangs. It had plenty of challenges, the lads were all pretty good about having a female boss, but they liked to keep me on my toes. Maybe these are stories for another day? Or another book?

Of course the highlight of the year was always the Christmas break-up functions. I used to try to get them out of town so as not to stir up the local population too much, as there is no doubt Forestry workers knew how to party. As long as we got them all home safely at the end of the night I was happy.

In the summer of 86/87 I had the opportunity to do a summer season at Scott Base, Antarctica. Just prior to heading south we were informed that the Forest Service was going to cease to exist the following year, a huge shock for all of us and an extra worry for me as I was genuinely concerned as to how this would affect all the guys I had working in my gangs. I was so eager to head to 'The Ice' that I didn't really care about my own job at that time, but of course towards the end of my time down there I had to start applying for jobs in the new entities. I guess for me it was fortuitous as now I really had the opportunity to head into the field I wanted to, Recreational Forestry. I was fortunate to pick up a position in Dept. of Conservation (DoC), working in the Catlins, then on to Nelson Lakes / Kahurangi, based in Murchison, before ending up in the Christchurch Conservancy Office. By then I had met my husband and once we decided to start a family together, I found my job not an easy one to juggle with him away a lot, so I resigned. I guess that's a sadness I carried for a long time, I had truly loved all of my career in the NZ outdoors, especially that time in the Forest Service. DoC did not manage to engender that same camaraderie between work mates as the good old NZFS!

I spent the last 22 years working part time as an Animal Control Officer (Dog Ranger), for Tasman District, and it was always a bit of a joke that my Ranger days seemed to head steadily downhill, from Forest Ranger to DoC Ranger and then to the Dogs!

Like many of my compatriots from those early Forest Service days our bodies are now paying the price for all that hard physical work, arthritis, shoddy knees, broken fingers and a few scars from sharp things, but yes, if I could do it all again I would. I had some great bosses over the years, so I quickly forgot the one who said those fateful words on my first day at Ashley! I don't see my ex workmates much these days, but when we do there are always plenty of yarns, laughs and some liquid lubrication to be had.

## Chris Bennett.

I laboured for a year at Otago Coast Forestry at Taieri Mouth in 77 before I joined the Woodsman School. I was a Woodsman in 78 and 79 at Berwick and then I went on to Tapanui and Tuatapere. I did some time at the Forestry base at Wyndham, then logging at Tapanui. It was a three year apprenticeship, I did my first two years at Berwick, then I got transferred to Wyndham, which was the headquarters for the Catlins Forest Park. It was mainly Silviculture work, then on to Tuatapere which was native forest. We did Cruising work at the Blue Cliffs beach for the Maori lands. I was also doing a lot of surveying work for new roads, plus a lot of scrub cutting.

I had to spend about two weeks in Lindsay & Dixons mill at Tuatapere, mainly log scaling. They are still cutting Beech there today. Berwick was opened after Dusky closed, they were two different schools. The first Woodsman Training School was at Dusky and after it closed the Woodie school was set up at Berwick. Dusky was at the back of Tapanui, heading towards Herriot. Berwick Forest is past the Berwick Township out past the Dunedin Airport. The huts and cook house are all still there. Our intake was about 11 or 12 Woodsmen, when I started there were only five, or maybe 6, second year guys there. In the first few months we had two or three leave out of our intake, I'm not sure why, but there were so few second year lads that there was very little bullying, just a little bit of hazing when we first got there. Standard stuff really, getting hosed down, tipped out of bed on the first night and that was pretty much the end of it. A few intakes before us the bullying and the hazing was pretty rough, we got told about it but it was not like that for us.

Most of my Woodsmen friends won't know me as Tinker, I only got that nickname when I started with Forestry here at Owaka. I came here in 1980 and was here when Forestry ended in 1987. I transferred from Tuatapere to here (Owaka), and I then transferred to Department of Conservation (DoC). Here at Owaka we had the Catlins Forest Park, we also had Lands and Survey, as well as Forestry. We looked after huts and walking tracks. I had to apply for a job with the new DoC, but I was lucky. Several of us just rolled over straight from Forestry into DoC. I got the letter from Forestry telling me I was dismissed and could apply for the new job in DoC, a lot of the jobs and people were already pre-selected and I was lucky, I just walked straight in. There were a lot of Forestry positions removed, there were just no jobs for many of those guys in the new DoC. I loved the Forestry side of work and I still think there's a place for what was the Forestry.

Management struggled to make the change work though. Some of the high production areas had standing timber ready to be felled, here at Owaka we had only a small amount of standing timber ready, but the government couldn't sell the existing forests. They tried to set up different corporations and companies but just couldn't sell the idea. Eventually everything was sold at fire sale or bargain basement prices and the Forest Companies we now have came into existence.

During our first year as Woodies we had a road trip, using a Forestry bus, to travel around the South Island. We visited forests in every conservancy and every type of forestry operations. We called into Golden Downs, not only visiting forestry operations there, but also playing rugby. We were actually the first team to beat the Downs at rugby, that was in 1978. We went right up the West Coast, staying at Harihari, and we visited the FRI (Forest Research Institute) there. We went out and watched them planting the bogs (swamps), in Pink Pine.

In our 2nd year, Tom C, our OC, took us for a 3 week trip to the North Island. We drove to Picton, across Cook Straight and on to Kaingaroa Forest. We stayed in the Pink Palace, visited the Muripara railhead, toured all around a great big private forest, saw the Pacific logging trucks with 6 trailers, watched them cross the main road (SH1), and watched traffic on the highway being stopped for these log train giants.
They put a plane on for us and flew us around, five at a time, over all the Kaingaroa forest and surrounding areas, so we got to see everything from the air, including just how big it was. I was able to open the window of the plane and lean out taking photos, it was fantastic. We got a really good look around.

We used to do a lot of burn offs before we planted land in new pine seedlings. We don't do that any more.

Some of my Woodie mates were; Irish, Spider and Bert, who died in a climbing accident. His brother was a 2nd year. We spent quite a bit of time in EF (Environmental Forestry), where we did things like hunting, maintaining swing bridges, night shooting, it was all part of our training. When we were with EF we all had trips down the Greenstone (a river), up the Caples, living out of a pack, it was great training. Then we went over to Stewart Island, where we spent 3 nights at Freshwater, learned to make camp bread and bush cooking. We learned to re-tension the ropes on the swinging bridges, repairing tread plates and any other maintenance needed. We would go to the 'Chocolate Swamp', then spend a week at Mason's Bay with old Tim, helping him muster and shear the sheep. They landed planes on Masons Bay and we often went out gathering Paua, it was fabulous. I think Tim had the last permit to catch and hold Red deer on Stewart Island, I believe most of them were eventually destroyed.

I got into the seed collecting team, we went all over the place, often spending a week or more at Naseby, seed collecting in Douglas Fir. We used to do the Dunedin Gardens and the Queenstown Gardens, collecting seed from all the Redwoods and Sequoias. When doing the Sequoia's in Dunedin we were lifted up in cherry pickers, in other places we just climbed the trees. When we were ultra high pruning we sometimes swapped from tree to tree to tree, to save going up and down each time. We started chainsaw work with Canadiens, and then we went to Husky 280s then 380s then 480s.

We had a married couple, Jean and Joe T. who were our cooks in the cookhouse. They had several 'very warm' daughters, as we liked to describe them. The cooking was alright but really not. If all the baked beans didn't get eaten in the morning we had them again for lunch, and if they still didn't get finished we had them there for the next morning. They used to call Joe 'Toad', Jean was just called the battle-axe. One time the helicopter came in with some bosses, and the 'good tucker' always came out when the bosses came.

On one particular day, the boss who flew in said to Toad, "Have you seen what's written on your roof"? and Joe said, "I don't think there's anything written on my roof". The boss said "You'd best go out and have a look mate". Written across the roof, in big letters was 'toad wanks'.

Shit he was wild, he didn't even know how long it had been there.

We never lived in a hostel, we always had individual huts and as we weren't allowed to cook in our huts, when the cooks gave us a really crap meal we would all chip in a couple of bucks each and send someone to town, to the nearest fish and chip shop, they'd come back with 50 or 100 bucks worth of fish and chips and we spread that all around the cookhouse and sit down to a decent feed.

I remember once, they rounded up all these poor bastards in the Octagon at Dunedin. I think they must've been PEP workers (Project - Employment Programme?), or some such thing, and they brought them out to go release cutting, or pruning. So these guys arrived out at Berwick, having left the Octagon at 6:30am, and they were freezing cold when they got out here. They had been brought out in old ex-army RL Bedfords with canvas covers on them. Fold down wooden seats along each side. Half of them were not properly dressed for winter, let alone for the work they were going to be doing. All of us Woodies were standing around, waiting to take them out to the various blocks for whatever work was planned. One guy was shuffling along the wooden seat on his bum, obviously having trouble getting out of the truck. Once he hopped down we found out that he had two wooden legs. He was very keen to work and we took him out to the job, but he got very tangled up in every bit of bracken and blackberry. I've never felt so sorry for anyone in all my life. He didn't last long in the gang.

Our third year was great. We all got split up, some of us went to Wyndham, some to Tuatapere, some to Tapanui and once there we also got moved around the various single mens camps. One camp had 8 rooms, 4 either side of a corridor, with an ablution block and kitchen. In one place we each had our own individual huts, but other people stayed there as well, such as shearing gangs. When we went to Tapanui we had a three bedroom house, it was brand new. At Tautari we again had our own individual huts, but each hut had its own kitchenette and bedroom. Those huts are still there today, but I think they might be a Backpackers accomodation now.

I loved it. All the little towns were ‘full noise’, always very busy. When Forestry closed up those little towns all died. We also got the winter employment guys, mainly from the Freezing Works. They came and did a whole lot of work for us, planting, pruning, whatever needed doing. At one time I was doing the timesheets for 118 guys. A lot of them were cutting the track lines through the native bush, they got paid good bonuses for that work. I was a Leading Woodsman at that stage.

There was a big blow in about 82 which flattened half of Balmoral forest. They were calling for guys from all over the place to go and help knock all the wind blow down. So lots of people from lots of forests went.

We did a lot of controlled burns and also a lot of firefighting. Late in 76 we went to a big burn at Hanmer. One night I got a phone call, we took all our gear to Momona Airport (Dunedin), where everything was loaded into a DC3 aeroplane. Pumps, hose packs, all our gear, us, everything was in.

And when we took of, rather steeply, it all slid to the back of the plane. Nothing had been tied down. Including us. When we landed we were picked up by the army, they took us out to the burn, they fed us, looked after us while we fought the fire. It was the first time I've ever seen Raro in a tin, they gave us little army can openers and we all got the shits because they didn't tell us we were supposed to water it down. The army would come around in these big old RL Bedford's, feeding us out of hotboxes off the tail deck of the trucks. We worked at that fire with beaters and shovels, that was our lot. I've never seen so many helicopters in all my life. We had U Drive jet boats for getting all our gear across the lake.

I remember we had a rifle called a Daid (Daide?) gun which was used to light fires. It fired a large cartridge with an inner container of phosphorus. From memory, firing it lit a fuse, which then detonated the phosphorous after it had hit the target area. It could be fired from either the side of the road into a patch of shrubbery, or from a helicopter down into a patch of bush or a gully that we wanted lit. The cartridge exploded, the phosphorus stuck to anything and everything and it would set fire to whatever it hit. I think that rifle is now in the Geraldine Museum.

## John Currie.

I grew up in Charleston, and went to primary school there. As there was no bus for secondary school kids I did correspondence school for a few years. At the end of my third form year my teacher in Wellington, a French guy, said; John's work is quite *unsatisfactory* in every respect. So that sort of indicated my academic career. By the time I was 14, I was running a possum trapping line with 65 traps and doing quite well, but my dad insisted I get an apprenticeship. He said that I had to go to town, that as long as my arsehole pointed to the ground I'd never be worth anything unless I had a career.

I remember going to a 'do' in town, in one corner were all the townie blokes in winkelpicker shoes and brylcream hairdos, talking about Buddy Holly and Elvis Presley, and in the other corner were a bunch of us country boys, trying on hobnail boots, sharpening knives, talking about going pighunting. Guess which group I was in?

I did get a job as a car spray painter, that didn't work out, and then for a while I had a bit of a stint in the railways as an apprentice shunter. It didn't work out either, so my mum found me this job at Golden Downs. All my uncles were bushmen or shooters and my dad didn't want that, so for me Golden Downs was an escape. I started at the Downs in 1958, nearly all our instructors were pommie bastards, that didn't go down well for a lot of the guys, even though we were kids.

I was born in the bush and I lived in the bush pretty much all my life. When I left for the Downs it was a hell of a thing for me, I thought I was going to the other side of the world. When I hopped on the Newmans bus, Mum gave me a hug and a little 'Baby Brownie' camera and while she stood by me to say goodbye, she said "Johnnie, you're gonna have an interesting life, take lots of photos". Which I did.

When I first went to the Woodsman school we used to have to run the length of the corridor and get whipped with knotted sheets. And get the shit beaten out of you. I remember there were two jokers standing on opposite sides of the corridor, in doorways with a sheet lying flat on the floor. When I came charging along, they lifted the sheet up quickly and I ran into it, quickly coming to a halt. Then they pulled the sheet taut and I went flying backwards, unable to keep my feet. Bloody and bruised, lying on the corridor floor wasn't much fun. I also got tied naked to a tree by the river, half an hour of the mossies and sandflies biting me was more than enough. For some reason I ended up covered in boils. The Welfare Officer's wife took me over to her place twice a week, ran a hot bath for me, and had me soaking in mustard to get rid of the boils and stop it hurting.

One of our instructors decided to take a couple of us lads pig-hunting. He said "Go down to the kennels and get out these 4 or 5 dogs, get them ready". He turned up with an old 'hearse' type of vehicle and told us to put the dogs in the back. Then he made us get in with the dogs. We were crapping ourselves, the dogs were growling, fighting and shitting, and we were stuck in it. But we got to go pig hunting.

One of our instructors, a raucous sort of a guy that we called Swindels, was hard to get along with. I remember playing a prank on him. We were up the south side of Long Gully. Swindels was driving us around in an OLB Bedford, when he got stuck. He made us fetch and carry rocks to put under the wheels to help get out. Then he made all the lads help to push him out, except when he tried to go forward, we pushed backwards, and when he tried to go backward, we pushed forward. He never clicked to what we were doing, after a hard half hour of fun he finally got the truck unstuck.

I really wanted to be a Culler, not a Woodsman, and was all set to go to the Hunter School. I actually went there, along with a few others. One guy turned up in a suit and tie and pointy leather shoes, with a briefcase. The instructor, Jim O. said, "You're never going to make a hunter" and sent him straight home.

Out in the bush one day chopping into an old rimu log, and I found some huhu grubs. I had four Maori chaps with me from the North Island and none of them had ever seen a huhu, let alone eaten one. I showed them how, and invited them to try, but they all vigorously declined. They decided to call me Abo Jack and that nickname has stuck with me.

I left the Downs and came back to became a Bushman at Charleston because dad bought a farm out on the beach and so I had to come home to manage and then buy the Brown's Terrace farm where I grew up.

My brother Val and I started the Mitchell Gully gold mine. It was a working gold mine but I wanted it to be a tourist attraction, so we built it with that in mind. We actually got a design award from the government, it was the first commercial tourist venture in the district.

One day a young teenage boy, Peter M, came over to me and said "there are a dozen goats on Allen's hill behind your farm and if you agree to take me up there, my boss said he'll lend me his rifle". I told him to come back when there were 18 or 20 goats. About a month later he told me there were about 20 goats. I'd been watching for them also and had been counting. We went up the north side of the hill and came around the corner into the goats, and they were there just in front of us, about 50 yards away, feeding around the hill. There was a big rock with a small gap, just big enough for me to get comfortable in, and so I set Peter up a bit off to one side. I said "I'll give you five minutes to get ready, then I'll start shooting". After I shot about the fourth or fifth goat I still hadn't heard a shot from Peter, I thought, 'he's got a jam'. But the goats were getting away so I couldn't muck around. I kept shooting. Then sometime later, I came to, lying on the ground, the whole side of my head felt like it had been blown away. As I came to, and I don't know how long it took me to get my senses back, Peter was crying and screaming for me to wake up.

My head was ringing, my hearing was gone, my head felt like it was bleeding everywhere, only there was no blood. Peter had come and stood just behind me with the muzzle of his .303 a couple of inches behind and to one side of my ear, and fired at the goats. I ended up getting an ACC payout, $7,000, which I didn't think was enough as other guys were getting $27,000 for their hearing losses. I've never got any hearing back in that ear.

I've had a great life, been married several times, had 5 kids, and I've got 15 grandkids and 13 great grandkids. I acquired quite a bit of extra land next to what I originally bought from my folks, and for a while I did tourist visits to the Nile Caves, which I was credited with finding, but I didn't, I just organised the first group of scientists (including Ornithologist Ron S.), who took away 10 big boxes of Moa bones from there. I also organised the first tour groups to the caves. There are some films done by the National Film Unit about the Moa bones we recovered from these caves, and we also found a complete Tuatara skeleton, which at the time was the furthest south that Tuatara had been discovered. The Film unit also made a movie of Deer Hunting in the Mohikinui, I led them in and guided the whole group.

I ended up gifting all that land (700 acres), that the Nile Caves are on, back to the crown. The Gold mine is still there but it stopped being a commercial venture when 'carless days' were introduced and we've never got it going again.

It's been an interesting life, and it's not done yet. I'm going to write a book and make my own movie, as soon as I learn to handle these electronic devices.

**Bo.**

I was in the 1975 intake at Kaingaroa Woodsman Training School. I remember being dropped off at the Hamilton bus station by my mother and grandmother, dressed in my all my best gear, along with an old battered suitcase, bound for Rotorua. I arrived to find an old Bedford gang bus with a bunch of young fellows hanging around. The driver, also our instructor, sent us off to wander around by ourselves and just make sure that we were back in time for the last trainees arrival. We were then taken to Kaingaroa, arriving at a very large two story hostel. The upper fire escapes were populated with second year trainees checking out the newbies.

The first thing we did was go off to the stores, to be issued with overalls and an axe (a Kelly axe I think). The overalls were highly modified and either the sleeves had been cut off, or the bottom half had been cut off to make a jacket of sorts. The pockets were always fair game to be torn off for use as toilet paper when need arose. Burning cigarette butts were often dropped into the unsuspecting trainees pockets, causing great hilarity and foul smells. I think most of us took up smoking upon arrival, as the canteen sold cigarettes. One gang boss tried to ban smoking in the gang bus on our way to and from work. We were so incensed by this that we decided to buy cigars. Our plan was to make a point. I don't remember if it was effective or not, but I do know how much smoke was produced. How anyone stood the amount of smoke I'll never know?

Our first job was axe thinning, three months of it. It was very hot on the volcanic plateau, and our hands were a bloody mess for most of the first few weeks until the callouses started to form. We also had to dig a number of rubbish holes, and the rubbish hole digging was turned into a competition between the different gangs, we achieved some great depths. Luckily, our thinning instructor liked reading 'yippee yarns' and once he had told us what to do, he pretty much left us alone. We were given strict instructions to ring bark any 'old crop' pines in amongst the block. These instructions were usually ignored and so then there had to be a separate operation (often many days), for several boys to bring these old pines to the ground with their newly gained axe skills. After the sound of the tree crashing down, the instructor would appear. A lot of time was spent throwing axes, or learning to throw axes. We had chopping races, cutting up old logs for huhu grubs. Plus, we eventually got the block thinned.

One of the better jobs we had was seed collection in old crop pine. We would climb as high as possible to hide out from the instructor. Once up in the thickest part of the canopy we would tie ourselves to the tree, and could then relax out of sight for awhile. Eventually we were told that once we had picked a large sack of cones we could knock off. This was great because we were working beside Kerosene Creek, which was a thermal river with some very nice hot pools for soaking in.

Life in the hostel was great. With a bunch of guys aged between 15 to 25 there was no end of fun. Food from the cook house was okay, but never enough for us growing lads so the canteen was very well patronised. Movies were shown twice a week, with second year trainees always doing the choosing. We had a very long run of Westerns and Kung Fu movies. Major Kung Fu fights always erupted after every movie. As everyone seemed to smoke, visibility was always a factor when watching movies. As young lads we were also always keen for any R18 movies but the occasional ones we got were mostly a disappointment. Most of the lads had enough Playboy and Penthouse posters on their walls anyway.

Cliff S. was our hostel 'guardian angel' and sports organiser. Many of us made ourselves scarce on rugby training nights, only to be tracked down by Cliff, saying "Come on son we need you". Memories of playing for the Woodsman rugby teams included playing out at Maunganui in the middle of nowhere, against some very large Bushman who wore boots and swannies. Old Māori ladies got involved and were always coming on the field to assist the referee. After match functions were always great.

Planting seemed to last for months, we had to chip away at the frozen pumice to be able to plant a tree in it. Many of us would succumb to the flu during the winter months, others pulled 'sickies' just to get a break from planting. Some even enlisted in the army for Basic Training, again, just to get out of planting. Some of my fellow trainees read somewhere that cough syrup was almost as good as alcohol, so a raid was carried out on the Matron's supply, with a large amount decanted off. After that the cough syrup was always under lock and key. As alcohol was a strict no-no for us we had to figure out ways of sneaking it in. The hostel manager's ears seemed to be attuned to the clank of bottles, so booze was only brought in when he was absent. Ruby Red wine was a favourite, one bottle was equal to two drinking sessions, it didn't take a lot at that age to put us on our ear.

Working in the logging gangs was the pinnacle for most of the trainees. Using chainsaws, felling trees, driving a log skidder or bulldozer was just great. Our instructor was very gruff and matter of fact, and from memory the most common instruction we got was mainly being told, "don't bloody-well cut yourselves". There were no chaps or other safety gear in those days. The instructor sometimes took us sheep rustling, he got us young lads to 'run down' a sheep for his freezer. It was considered okay because it was from the Lands and Survey block.

# Short Stories.

## Animal Control.

In the late 1950's the Forest Service took over control of noxious animal operations in New Zealand, resulting in a single men's camp being built at Blue Glen, at the back of King's Camp. This was to be the initial training ground for would be Deer Cullers. If the Woodsmen were successful at Blue Glen they then went to another camp at Dip Flat in the Lake Rotoiti area. Once you were there you were officially a Deer Culler.

We were taking stores in one Friday afternoon when we met a man running flat out towards us. He told us "a man's been shot, he's back at the camp". Taking him back to Blue Glen we found the patient with a massive hole blown through one thigh. He was very lucky, bone and artery were intact. He told us that he had shot a big stag earlier in the day, and had tied the head to his pack. Unfortunately, he tied it so that it was sticking up above his head. He was in a gully, in fairly thick young manuka scrub and going back to camp when a fellow trainee culler on the ridge above saw the antlers moving through the scrub. He fired where he thought the deer's body would have been. When he raced down to get his trophy he found he had put a bullet in one of his mates. Fortunately camp was close, and

because the radio wasn't working, he started running. We managed to get the patient on to the back of the runabout and got him back to headquarters and then on to Nelson hospital, where he spent quite some time having reconstructive surgery. His days as a Culler were over. It was his own bloody fault, we had all been repeatedly told that when you bring a stags head home, you tie the antlers *upside down* on your pack for carrying.

## Fats and the gold tooth.

In the winter of 71 after dinner one evening, a group of 1st year Woodies were standing along the corridor in the back hostel, leaning against the radiators, keeping warm before bedtime, scratching their balls and generally talking crap. Hapuka must have said something that annoyed Fats, because Fats just wandered along and gave Hapuka a good punch in the mouth, causing his much prized gold tooth to disappear down the corridor somewhere. Unfortunately, Hapuka had been fairly attached to this tooth, especially as his Mother had struggled to give it to him some 4 or 5 years earlier when, as a young boy he'd fallen and broken a front tooth in half. In a family of 8 kids a gold tooth and Dentist bills was a very expensive gift. Anyway, Hapuka disappeared into his room and emerged with a battle cry and his newly sharpened axe, which was ready for the next day's axe thinning. Charging down the corridor after Fats, who had quite properly read the tone of the moment and disappeared as rapidly as possible into his own room, slamming the door vigorously behind him. The axe slammed into the brass door handle, well and truly opening the door, allowing Hapuka to then behold Fats stuck and struggling in the open

window, going nowhere. Fortunately, sanity prevailed, a few moments later there was lots of laughter, Fats got himself unstuck, Hapuka went off to find his tooth and sharpen his axe (again), and the incident was over as quickly as it had come.

## How far will an arrow go?

The Duh returned home from Nelson one Friday night with a bow and arrow set. This was a very high quality piece of kit, probably the first archery equipment most of us had ever seen and Duh spent the week playing with it, setting it up and putting it away again. The following Friday night there were only a handful of Woodies still in camp (in the back hostel anyway), and Duh brought his bow out into the rec room. How many rooms do you reckon it would go through he asked. Some of us said don't be a Duh / dickhead. Some of us said, "depends on whether it hits a stud or not". Someone mentioned what if someone's in their room? So Duh, stringing his bow, stands at the end of the corridor and yells out loudly "Is anyone here?" No answer, so after having guessed where the studs in the rooms would be, Duh nocks an arrow, steps back into the corridor a few paces, draws and releases his arrow through the first bedroom on that side of the corridor. I don't really recall whether the rest of us were shocked that he'd actually done it. We worked our way along the corridor opening each door (no locks), and checked. A hole in both walls. On to the next room, holes in the walls. And so on, room 5, room 10, room 15, 16. Well, 16 rooms had a neat hole in both walls, in and out and the arrow was into the 16th room. If I recall correctly, there were 20 rooms down that side of corridor. They weren't all occupied, half of our intake had well and truly left by that stage but man, that could so easily have turned out so much worse than bad. Duh got renamed Super Duh from then on. That night quite a few magazines (Playboy and Penthouse probably), had pages ripped out and pasted up over the holes. It was many months before the hostel manager found out about it, and the SuperDuh was long gone by then. Maybe it was cheap ultra thin hardboard on the walls, or just the awesome power of a good bow.

## Soapy and the Citroen.

In the last half of 1963 in our 2nd year of training, Ray (from Warrington), Trevor (ex Wanganui), and myself went for a drive to Lake Rotoiti and of course the Tophouse Pub is on that route.

We decided to stop in and visit the smallest bar in the country, and were shown the bullet hole from an incident some years back. Now a decision was needed, what sort of alcohol to buy? I had tasted beer a couple of years previously when running around the Ohai and Nightcaps roads with some friends, and as I hadn't liked the beer taste back then, I chose a bottle of Blackcurrant Gin. I think I must have been talked into it by Ray and Soapy or the bar owner, as I certainly hadn't tasted it before. Maybe it sounded more like a soft drink? I can remember the cost was 18 shillings & sixpence. I think that converts to a $1.85 in today's money. Another car full of Woodsmen also made the trip, I can remember the car (a Chevvy), but not sure who was in it.

We arrived at the lake okay, and skylarked around a bit before Ray drove down near the shore and of course, being a 1948 Citroen it was front wheel drive and promptly got stuck in the gravel. A couple of us pushed and we were soon on our way back towards the Downs.

Somewhere, we stopped on the side of the road for a few drinks but soon felt that we'd be better off out of sight a bit, so we cruised up a fire break on the top of Kerr's Hill. We were soon joined by the other car load and we proceeded to drink and enjoy the sunshine.

We had a bit of a competition throwing rocks at a skinny tree down the side of the hill a bit (it didn't take much to amuse us in the condition we were getting in). I drank all my Blackcurrant Gin myself and was then getting handed a few beers. Now this is really my absolute first time having a fair bit of alcohol so I was getting pretty tiddly. Someone decided it was time to sneak back down Kerr's Hill (which was gravel, narrow and very sharp bends in those days). With tall forest all around, the road was quite wet and slushy. The 3 of us sat in the front with an old meat-paste glass of beer each. As Ray drove very carefully around a tight corner (beer in one hand), the car slid into and up the bank on the right hand side of the road. It was like slow motion as the car went up the bank and fell ever so gently on its side. I clearly remember moving my beer glass around to keep it upright, being careful not to spill my drink. Unfortunately Soapy, being in the middle, fell on my arm and spilled my beer! There were comments about my beer spilling prowess. Of course Ray who was driving, fell onto Soapy, so that's my excuse I suppose.

Now our task was for us to get the Citroen back on its wheels. Just as we were attempting to do this, a truck with a canopy on the back came around the corner. It was filled with Boy Scouts who had been on a camp somewhere. No problem, with their assistance the car was soon back on all 4 wheels and we drove back to the hostels. The Boy Scouts of course had done their 'good deed' for the day.

Phew, we got away with that one! Or so we thought. The next day we were called into Cliff K's (OC), office.

Well, we were each given a stern talking to and confined to camp for a month, which was actually very lenient at that time, because being caught with alcohol or having been drinking was a sackable offence. As Barney had found out in the intake before. He lost his job but was reinstated into our 62 intake the following year. As can be guessed, the Scouts had done another 'good deed' and reported to the Forest Service boss what they had

encountered.
I'm not sure what the other two guys did in their careers but I stayed with the NZFS until it was disbanded, so in total I did over 49 years in the Forestry, no regrets whatsoever. It was a great life.

## Oops!

Very early in my second year we were teaching 1st year Woodies how to thin some Douglas Fir that had been planted in the depression years and had never again been looked at. So, lots of undergrowth, lots of low branches, very difficult to work in, or to thin. We all had lots of hangups because the trees were so thick, and forestry instructions were that each hangup would be brought down by chopping the stem into short pieces, there was to be none of the 'climbing the stem and jumping on it till it fell' nonsense. This was often ignored as it tripled the amount of work we had to do, and if our instructor was away on the other side of the hill, what he didn't see didn't hurt him.

One of the first years, John C, felled a big tree and had a hangup, and didn't pay attention to the fact that the hangup was directly over some standing Manuka. John raced up the tree and started bouncing to get it to fall, which it did, but he fell into and broke some Manuka stems on the way down. We heard loud screaming and when we got there, John was standing on tiptoe, having impaled himself on a piece of broken off Manuka. The stick, thicker than my thumb had penetrated his groin, just behind two very delicate objects, and gone deep into his abdomen. We very quickly tied his legs together with the stick in place, sawed the stick off at ground level with a pruning saw, and transported him to Nelson Hospital. He survived with no permanent damage to any of his bits and pieces.

Sometimes it could be useful to fell many trees in a row, and if conditions were right, the weight of multiple trees falling could 'sort of' guarantee that no hangups would occur, a bit like a domino effect. So, one would scarf the first tree, then go to the next one back and do the same. And so on, for as far back as needed. Then, once all of your trees had been scarved, you'd go back down the hill to the first one and start to put in the back-cut, just enough so that the tree is almost ready to fall. Then quickly back to the next tree, do the back-cut, and so on until you have a couple, or six or a dozen trees ready to fall. Then the last and highest tree in the line is dropped, and as it falls, it takes down all the others with it. Like giant dominoes. There are some risks inherent in this, but when it works well it looks great. If the wind changes when you've got one tree ready to fall it's a problem, if it changes when you've got a dozen ready it's a disaster. And if you're fifty yards up the hill and another Woodie or the Instructor walks into the line of trees that you're about to drop, you need to do some very loud and quick yelling.

## In the dark of the night.

One of our intake came from a little village high up on the South Island's West Coast (Karamea), and being a small rural community, they had regular dances in the village hall. The possibility of lots of pretty girls, and a bit of dancing was too much to ignore. We decided to take a car load over on Saturday afternoon, planning to get there in time for the evening to start.

Snorkel's very early Ford Popular was definitely the most likely to make it there and back. In those days much of the road between Westport and Karamea was an unsealed goat track (I'm exaggerating a bit), and over the part known as the Karamea Bluff, it was a bit of a nightmare.

It was midwinter, raining heavily, early evening but dark already and as we drove over the Bluff a large mudslide / rockslide came down the hill and blocked the road ahead of us. We saw it happening and stopped in time, but the road was well and truly blocked. We were all in our best clothes,

we had planned on going straight to the dance. As we watched and pondered, cars also bound for Karamea started arriving behind us and before long, turning around and going back to Westport wasn't an option. Being capable young men (dumb, surely not?) we got out into the storm and stripped down to our undies. Almost naked and barefooted, in the car headlights, we moved rocks, boulders and mud, using our hands, feet and branches, whatever we could find. An hour later we had a 'sort of' track through the slip that we thought we could get the Popular through, with a bit of pushing and shoving. All the people waiting in the several dozen cars behind us declined to help, they just kept shouting for us to hurry up and clear the road. We were sworn at, laughed at, heckled and a few hardy souls even got out of their cars with umbrellas and watched us work and told us which rocks to move.

So by ourselves, we struggled and grunted and got the car through. Then, because we'd had enough of the heckling (and because we could), we climbed back up onto the slip and encouraged a few more rocks and debris to fall down onto the road, effectively blocking it again. We saw the funny side but the people waiting behind us didn't, a lot of swearing came our way. We were filthy, mud covered, so we washed as best we could in all the little waterfalls pouring down the high side of the road, and drove to Karamea in our undies, where we showered and dried at our mate's parent's place, and then went on to the dance. We had a wonderful evening, stayed for breakfast and lunch on Sunday, Hapuka's mum cooked us the best bacon and eggs and toast that I've ever had, I can still taste that breakfast. Then on back to the Downs. Lucky for us, the Ministry of Works chaps had cleared the slip over the Bluff and we were able to drive straight home to Golden Downs in time for work on Monday morning.

## Wasps.

New Zealand has its fair share of imported (and now unwanted), critters and the German Wasp must be one of the worst.

Late in 1973, a group of us were 'Timber Cruising' on the West Coast near Nelson Creek, not far from Totara Flat where we were based. Timber Cruising is the method used to determine how much millable timber is in a particular block or area of land. Generally, this would be native forest, so Kaihikatea, Rimu, Rata, Matai, Miro, etc., and generally, this land is not accessible by vehicles. So the Woodsmen drove to the nearest road access, then walked into the block each day. This could be a trek of maybe up to 10 km, through native bush and generally very hilly terrain. We ran in first thing in the morning, we ran out last thing at night. We carried packs, lunches, slashers, and all other tools, including occasionally, a chain saw or crowbar. In earlier years the Cruisers stayed in the bush for a week or 10 days at a time so they had it a lot tougher than we did.

To begin, a given area is divided into grid squares, and tracks are cut to divide the entire block into equal size squares, much like a chess board. Then each tree in a given square is identified (species), and each tree is numbered, measured, recorded. Various tools and techniques are used to measure the tree's dimensions, the height, the diameter at breast height, etc, and all these measurements are taken from the ground with no damage being done to the tree. Occasionally a bit of loose bark or supplejack vine might be removed to give a better tape measure reading. Various calculations then give the volume of timber in a particular log and that information is then used by the forest owners to determine possible future logging operations or whatever else they may decide.

Often we would be in a particular block for many weeks and would use the same track in, changing the tracks as required, as parts of the block were finished and new areas were opened up to work on. If we had enough people, some would be cutting tracks and grid lines, some would be measuring trees in the grids, etc.

On one part of a track we found a large wasp nest, but if we jumped it as we ran past, by the time the wasps came out of the nest we were all safely away down the track. On the way out at night we just did the same jump, no problem. One just had to remember where the nest was.

Anyway, each summer we were allocated a number of university students

to work with us, presumably for them to see if they liked Forestry as a possible career and potentially go on to Ranger School. One particular student was a bit of a loud mouth and very derogatory towards Woodsmen. It was decided that he needed taking down a peg or two. Someone came up with the bright idea of putting a log in front of the wasp nest. We all made sure to jump well over the wasps but the poor student running his butt off to keep up with us landed right on the wasp nest. None of us, including our Instructor had ever dealt with wasp stings or Anaphylactic Shock but we learned in a hurry that day. Two things saved that lads life that day. We had a stretcher made from 2 Manuka poles and two swannies in a matter of minutes, and between six of us, we ran non-stop carrying him back to the truck and had him in hospital within the hour. He literally swelled like a balloon. It was supposed to be a practical joke and a lesson. I don't know if he ever realised it was deliberate, I hope not.

## Outward Bound.

As a 4th year Woodsman in Waipoua Forest Kauri Sanctuary, my job was tallying the timber on the skid sites of the private logging contractors who were logging the exotic timber in the sanctuary.

The job wasn't very demanding, I had plenty of time to spare, so I just grabbed the odd chain saw that was lying around and began limbing and cutting to length the logs brought down to the skids by skidders and bulldozers. Before long, in addition to my own forestry duties I was doing all of the skid work for the contractors (unpaid), unhooking strops from logs, measuring and cutting the logs and trimming limbs which had been missed on the hillside. Of course this impressed my Forestry bosses because the logging contractor (Bernie G), was also pretty happy with what I was doing. Forestry was so impressed that they offered me a position (all expenses paid), to the Outward Bound School at Anakiwa. I was all set to go when Bernie came to me one evening and said that if I quit forestry immediately and came to work for him full time, he would teach me to drive a log skidder and, in a years time, when he purchased what was then going to be NZ's biggest log skidder (a Clark C7D), I would be it's driver.

I accepted, immediately resigned from the Forest Service and yes, I learned to drive a small International skidder, and then, eventually, the C7D.

I loved driving skidders, it was such exciting work. The hills were steep, the job potentially dangerous, physically demanding, real 'man's work' but I was still just a teenage boy. Now at over 70 years old, one of the few decisions I've regretted in my life was NOT going to Anakiwa.

## Gus remembers.

I was in the 63 intake, I remember not being allowed to have my car there in the first year (they locked it up), so I had to learn how to break into it and steal my own stuff whenever I needed to get away.

One of my intake was a guy we called SamiSamo, a son of Samoan royalty who was sent to learn about Forestry and was supposed to take his knowledge back home but, apart from a couple of holidays, he never took his skills home.

I really remember the hard work, especially at fires. We'd need water a mile up a hill so we'd carry a portable canvas dam up a hill, then fill it using a Wajax pump and hoses from a creek at the bottom of the hill. Then another pump, more hoses leading to another dam another couple of hundred yards up, and so on as far as we needed to go. The dams were heavy, the pumps were heavy, petrol cans were heavy, the hoses were heavy and it was always uphill. But we got the water everywhere it was needed. I went to Totara Flat (West Coast), and did Timber Cruising and then on to Conical Hill where all we did was grade timber. I helped build a runway up on Mount Arthur but after we'd finished it and the first plane came in, they didn't have space for us, so they made us walk home.

I also remember how dangerous a lot of the work was. We did some ultra-high pruning once, where we were working so high the only way to get high enough was to climb the ladder, then once we reached the top of the ladder we climbed onto a branch and pulled the ladder further up the tree, tying it on. Sometimes we were working over 120 feet up. No safety gear. One of the stories that I'm not so keen on remembering was one of the guys was considered to be a bit effeminate. Maybe he was a 'poofter?' He got attacked in the showers and some toothpaste was squeezed up his bum. He left that night and never returned.

## Fire Station.

Vi & Sonny were working in the Fire Dept, cleaning hoses. This back breaking work was necessary after every fire where hoses or pumps had been used, thousand and thousands of feet of hose needed scrubbing and hanging up on the hose tower to dry. They had a couple of 1st years with them learning the job and the chain of command wasn't working too well, the 1st years weren't doing as they had been asked… or told. So they were tied at the top of the tower with ropes and told that they'd be released when they'd been punished enough.

Some time later, Vi & Sonny got the guys off the tower, down to the water hole and then threw them both into it.

Only one resurfaced!

Sonny panicked, jumped in to save the missing lad, only to have him resurface, having held his breath for as long as he needed to, to panic Vi & Sonny, to see them get wet too!

## Butt.

We were in a South West Coast hotel when Jack A. got punched by Horse. Horse was so called because his christian and surname initials were GG, so obviously he was either called Horse or GG, or sometimes just

Giddyup. Horse had fallen asleep leaning against the bar and Jack decided to play a practical joke on him. Someone had almost finished a smoke, so Jack put the still burning butt in Horses ear. Someone said "that might be lethal". Everyone was watching as the ciggy smouldered away, till Horse awoke with a yell. He jumped up, looked around and without asking or saying anything, just punched Jack an almighty haymaker. Jack fell to the floor, said "I knew that would be fatal", before lapsing into oblivion. Horse just went back to sleep leaning on the bar.

## Fireworks.

Golden Downs had a nice rugby field and in the weeks before Guy Fawkes, it was possible to have a large selection of fireworks, sky rockets and other items that would go bang in a spectacular fashion.

On a number of occasions I've seen (and been part of), groups of Woodsmen at opposite ends of the field, using empty beer bottles as rocket holders, lighting and firing sky rockets at the group standing under the goal posts at the other end of the field.

Although it sounds dangerous, a 100 yards is a long way and the flight time of a skyrocket over that distance is well sufficient to allow the guys at opposite ends to take evasive action. Gravity usually had the rockets sliding along, at or near ground level and so it's easily possible to just jump, either up or sideways as the rocket approaches. Just a test of reflexes really. To make it really interesting, sky rocket ballistics aren't as precise as one might like, so occasionally, rockets would veer suddenly, left or right, down into the grass or skywards, who would know? One needed to keep one's eye on the ball, so to speak. That could result in a bit of last second evasiveness at the target end of the field, with the jocularity and derision that would follow. For some reason that I still can't fathom, these activities never got any attention from the powers that be. I never saw anyone hurt in any way doing these madcap things but perhaps that was more by good luck than good management.

## A spot of poaching.

One winters evening in 71, a couple of 2nd year Woodies at the Downs decided to go for a hunt. Spotlighting was of course illegal within Golden Downs. They set off in an old Ford V8 ute and a short time later, were followed out of the village by a couple of 1st year guys who wanted to get in on the action and do a bit of shooting themselves. The 2nd year guys saw the lights following them and assumed that it was a Ranger coming to catch them in the act, and so they put pedal to the metal. A bit fast around one corner saw the ute fail to take the curve and deposit itself neatly on its side just off the road. No one was hurt in the roll over, but as both guys got out of the vehicle they realised the .303 was still inside the cab. Both reached in from opposite sides of the cab to grab the rifle and a shot fired. The bullet passed through the roof of the cab and then into Rat's neck. The bullet (a military FMJ) had split into two pieces as it went through the steel cab and both bits were still together as they entered Rat's neck but they separated a bit and came out on the opposite side of his neck in two separate holes. The following car was just stopping, they had seen the rollover and heard the shot. Almost immediately the first years guys were on the scene and so Rat was bundled into the other car and with a finger in each of the holes, stopping the blood, he was hurriedly taken back to Golden Downs where Matron was still on duty, just about to close her clinic for the night. She took over, Rat was taken to hospital. He survived and I don't know what happened after the incident to those involved, I know I was never questioned about it. There were some very lucky people that night.

## Pumpkins.

Many intakes had a liking for making their own booze, and fermented pumpkin juice was super easy to make (eat your heart out Harry Potter). Many guys from various intakes have told me their versions, this was ours. We found some pumpkins, cut the top out neatly and hollowed them out, then filled the cavity with raisins, cranberries, sultanas, chopped up apples, whatever fruit we could find, added a bag of sugar, mixed it well, added a bit of water to top it off and put the lid back on. We sealed ours with melted candle wax, and then being the innovators that we were, we excavated a hole in the creek (well below normal water level), behind the second year huts, dropped the pumpkins in and then covered the hole back in with all the rocks and gravel that had come out. Regular checks for a while to make sure the hole wasn't washing out, then we forgot about it.

Six or eight months later, we remembered, and once the pumpkins were recovered and opened, well, we had a great time. That stuff was lethal, and so very, very tasty. I know other intakes buried their pumpkins under their little gardens, or just hid them under a hut somewhere. Who ever wondered about the silly drunken Woodsmen wandering around on a fine Saturday morning?

## Not just guys.

A Women's gang was set up in Rankleburn Forest and mainly consisted of the wives of the wage workers.

I believe they all travelled over from Tapanui where the District Office was situated. I was sent over from Otago Coast Forest on secondment as acting Second in Charge (2IC), over an Autumn / Winter period.

The then OC came out in his truck, introduced himself and then proceeded to show these ladies how to low prune trees. The stand of Radiata was un-thinned and to my trained experience, was borderline needing to be high pruned. However he knew best. When he left I called the ladies together and showed them the actual correct way to hold and use their Porta Pruners. They were also given Jacksaws for the larger branches. With the ladies not yet having a lot of upper body strength they were encouraged to swing on the handles back and forward and use even pressure, hence making it a lot easier to cut the limb.

Before they started, they were told that overalls would be issued after they had been on the job a month, but after a couple of weeks they started complaining about blackberry and gorse ripping their clothing. I did say to them not to try and climb through the blackberry, but to try and avoid it where possible, walk around it if they could. Before the month was up and well before they got any overalls, I found that I couldn't handle the constant whining. I gave the job of supervising the ladies over to a younger Woodie.

## Sucked in!

Three days into my first year, safely tucked up in my bed, almost asleep and all of a sudden someone is screaming "Fight, fight, fight".

With the crashing sounds of many dozens of pairs feet racing down the corridor, I joined the stampede and raced out the back of the hostel. As soon as we exited the building, the five or six second year guys on the roof started tipping buckets of water over us and other second years on each side sprayed us with fire hoses. Apparently the lads in the other hostel got the same treatment at the same time.

## Horses.

There were many forests around NZ where logging with horses was done, and in the early years at Golden Downs it was part of the Woodsman syllabus. The horses were mainly used for production thinning of 10 – 12 year-old trees, which were being felled to achieve final tree spacing. These logs were destined to be posts, strainers and poles. Ian L. told me about how some of the new Woodsmen who had previously worked with horses were excellent, but many of the boys had no idea and were never going to be much use around horses. The biggest requirement was patience. Working with horses and trying to instil into trainee Woodsmen the relaxed methods needed to manage the horses was always going to be a big ask.

Horses were also used on some of the tracks. We used 3 horses on the Heaphy Track as pack horses, to carry in bags of cement, coils of wire rope and other heavy supplies when we couldn't get these things choppered in. Some these horses were very easy going but some were cantankerous. One horse in particular had to be loaded very carefully, if the load was even a little off balance or lopsided, the horse would deliberately bang into the trees on that side of the track until he had either dislodged or levelled up his load. In hindsight, I think that horse was smarter than we were.

## Ross sandwiches.

Making 100 plus lunches 5 days a week cannot have been easy. Our cook used a sort of a weakened margarine, we all reckoned it was mixed with something like milk in order for it to be easily spread, it was a white spread and was put on with a couple of swipes of a paint brush. The fillings were mainly baked beans, jam, lettuce, marmite and a processed meat, Belgian roll, called luncheon these days. All these products made for easy and fast to make lunches.

We got sick of them pretty quickly, but we were also always hungry so we ate them. Funnily enough we got sick of the tasteless meat roll we called horsecock or dogcock first.

In Golden Downs there was a Forester called Ross W. who went to work every day, even weekends. While out hunting somewhere, many of us would come across Ross beavering away on various plot work or some related technical stuff, his vehicle could always be seen going or parked somewhere. I do not remember who made the connection of Ross being out there every day and us getting luncheon sandwiches every day but the luncheon sandwiches became known as Ross Sandwiches from that point onwards.

## The Boathouse.

Around the time that Teddy Boys, Bodgies and Widgies started to become the thing in the UK, a lot of Kiwi lads started to copy the UK boys. In our first year at the Downs we went with a bus load of second and third year Woodsmen to The Boathouse in Nelson. The venue seemed to have an over abundance of Teddy boys and the Nelson lads decided that Woodies weren't welcome. A rumble started when the Woodsmen arrived, soon spilling out onto the balcony overlooking the water. Several of the Woodies were 3rd and 4th years, a lot bigger and stronger than the local lads, a couple of whom got thrown over the railing. Unfortunately for them, the tide was out so it was just a rocky beach which became their landing pad. Multiple contusions and a couple of broken bones resulted, and the Woodies weren't welcome back in The Boathouse for quite awhile after that.

## Getting trout the hard way.

Working on the Heaphy track in 1971, Sparrow, Matt D. and John B. were left to their own devices when their boss, Pete DV, was away in Greymouth or some such place, getting a new set of teeth. He'd left us alone (with a bit of work to do), and a Karamea local, Billy Half-foot, was travelling in and out of the Heaphy and Lewis huts with pack horses and White-baiting gear. For a spot of cash, Billy agreed to bring some beer (5 flagons and some spirits), in on one return trip. The resulting alcoholic haze resulted in John B. getting alcohol poisoning and he had to be choppered out. The chopper was being used to ferry hut building supplies into the track and the pilot, John R. was parked at the Heaphy hut on down time, so John B was lucky.

Billy wasn't a Woodsman, but along with Normy No-Fingers who was, they'd both removed various parts of their own anatomy, by using small pieces of explosive and detonators for the acquisition of trout. In Billy's case, a lit piece of fuse and small sliver of explosive was hurriedly dropped to the ground when a Ranger appeared from behind a bush, asking "What the hell do you think you're doing?" Stamping on the burning fuse didn't extinguish it, and so Bill changed his surname from that day on.

Pretty much the same with Norm, except he just held the charge behind his back. Ow! It was also pretty common to use 'nickel spinners' or the 'hydro minnow' (.303 cartridges), to acquire eels or trout. It was about as legal then as it would be now.

The Motueka river behind the back hostel wasn't only a great place to swim. A favourite place where 'hard up' Woodies who couldn't afford fly

rods and fishing licences used the trusted 'nickel spinner' as an alternative means of catching a feed.

## Movie Night.

Then there was Baldy, JC & Trevor W.
On more than one occasion, a Forestry bus which was usually parked outside the office, was used very quietly to get 'some of us' out of the camp. This particular night was a film night at the Downs, and I remember that 'The World of Suzie Wong' was playing.

Instead of watching the movie, a few of us chose to go travelling by 'borrowing' the gang bus. Into Wakefield, Belgrove, a bit of shopping, buy a bit of booze, and home. On our return trip to the Downs, we came back into camp very quietly, stopping to reconnect the speedo, which was always disconnected before leaving, for obvious reasons.

However that night, the film projector had broken down, the movie stopped early, and the Kings Camp crew were returning home early because of the breakdown. As they went home, they came across the gang bus parked on the road, just as we were getting the speedo reconnection done. The King's Camp crew started slowing down to check out the vehicle i.e, obviously not where it was supposed to be.
JC, without hesitation, gave them a wave, jumped back into the bus and took off before they could fully stop and could check what was going on.

We also, at times, took the bus to Nelson and sometimes fuel became an issue because we'd spent what little cash we'd had. Usually pissed as chooks, there were times we needed fuel to return. Off we would go to 2nd hand car dealer places, milk any petrol tanks that we could and solve our problem.

## Movie Night 2.

One of our Woodies (Larry H), who was a very big lad, also very well built, had got into a spot of bother with the law in Dunedin. They gave him a choice; Go to the Woodsman School or go to Borstal. He planned to stay at the Downs only long enough for the heat at home to die down a bit before heading back for home. He found himself in a pub on Collingwood Street (Nelson), and the clientele were a pretty hard bunch. Somehow he managed to get into a bet requiring him to run naked around the block. As there was £25 (yes, pounds, 3-4 weeks wages), up for grabs, he decided to go for it. He stripped stark bollocky in the bar, leaving all his kit on the floor in front of the bar. He headed out the door, towards the Royal pub at a gallop, hung a left along Bridge Street to the center of town, left onto Trafalgar Street, just as the picture theatre was emptying out. He ran straight through the mob of movie goers, towards the Cathedral, then another left onto Hardy Street, left again onto Collingwood Street and then onto the home straight and back to his clothes. After getting dressed, he collected his winnings and shouted the bar. Marvellous stuff.

## Hot spot.

Sometime in mid 1974 (autumn / winter) there was a Controlled Burn somewhere in the Golden Downs Forest. It was a smallish, 50 hectare block, surrounded by firebreaks and outside that, standing forest surrounding the entire burn block. I was a 3rd year Woodie and was part of a large team who were going to light and manage the burn. It was decided that because of the nature, location of, and ground slash conditions, it would be an ideal block to light the entire perimeter at once, or as fast as possible. Lots of guys with flame wands, several fire engines with flame throwers, all starting at the top of the hills and working their way down the firebreaks. I think it took about half an hour to get the entire perimeter lit, and then an amazing thing (amazing to me, anyway), happened. If you can imagine a wall of fire surrounding a block of land (mainly one big hillside) and the fire started behaving or looking like a fiery waterspout or tornado. The entire wall of fire just seemed to suck in towards the center of the block from all directions. The force of this 'cyclone' of fire caused whole logs to be pulled into the air where they just whirled around, burning in the ever more intense center of the burn. The logs and other burning debris were pulled hundreds of feet in the air and just spun in place. I've always regretted not having a camera, but I was too busy working. From the entire perimeter the fire just swept in, the heat and the intensity had to be seen to be believed. I don't think I've ever seen a more successful burn; Fire Management obviously knew what they were doing.

## Not getting away with it.

We didn't always get away with some of the shit that we did. Snorkel always had it in for Goober. We all picked on each other, and every opportunity to give someone a hard time was always exploited. But some of us just didn't get on well and sometimes things went to extremes. During their 3rd year at Totara Flat, Snorkel was not happy with something Goobs had done, or probably, and much more likely, Snorkel was just being a dickhead. Snorkel emptied a shotgun shell of powder and pellets, then loaded the now 'blank' cartridge into his gun and barged into the Rec room, ranting that he was going to shoot Goobs. When he pointed the gun and fired the blank at Goober, we all shat ourselves. Very unfairly, some of us laughed at the prank. Snorkel got six months probation from Forestry Management for this and obviously had to keep his nose clean from then on.

## The Drover's Dream.

Many of us at Totara Flat had the pleasure of working with Andy K. Andy used to travel considerable distances on his old pushbike, especially on weekends, visiting the wealth of hotels we had available. Now Andy was a fine singer and had a repertoire of good songs, one of his favourites was the Drovers Dream. One evening returning home from a rugby game at Reefton, we saw Andy's bike lying on the side of the road. When we stopped, all we could hear was a loud rendition of the Drovers Dream, coming from somewhere. We couldn't see Andy, but eventually found him lying on his back in a deep ditch, singing his little heart out. It turned out that he'd had an argument with a mob of sheep and the sheep won. When he couldn't get out of the ditch he decided to sing. We loaded him and his bike into the truck and took him home to Ahaura for a well deserved sleep before going home ourselves.

## Baby Possum.

One of our crew killed a possum one night and then kept the infant possum that had been clinging to her back. He kept it in his room and he made diapers for it to keep the mess to a minimum. Every evening our Matron, Mrs. C, did her rounds of the hostel, talking to the boys, making sure everyone was Ok. One evening, not quite dark yet, there was a huge thunderstorm and the baby possum, scared by the thunder and lightning, came running out of its room dressed in its diaper. Matron, walking along the corridor saw it, screamed "a Rat" and turned and ran. Just then, lightning hit the main transformer near the camp, there was a huge bang, and all the lights went out as Matron was running along the corridor. The baby possum made for the nearest tall object (matron), and scarpered up her legs, onto the top of her head where it got its claws firmly in her hair. Now almost dark, with Matron screaming blue murder, the possum started pissing itself. It seemed to take forever to rescue that possum.

## Conical Hill.

We had a guy at Conical Hill, a tally clerk by the name of Des C. Des was wider than he was tall and a real piss-head. At the time he would have been between 50 and 60 years old. One night he drove back from the pub so pissed that after he parked his car in the covered parking bay, he simply passed out behind the wheel. We got quite a few guys and managed to pick up his car (a hillman imp I think), and turn it around so that it was parked sideways in the shed. There wasn't a lot of wiggle room to manoeuvre it and it was bloody heavy with Des in it, but eventually, with a bit of too-ing and fro-ing and kangaroo hopping, we had the car sideways. Des spent months trying to figure out how he parked it like that before someone told him.

## Block 22.

Two hunters from Balclutha turned up on my doorstep one day and told me that they'd lost their mate. It had been snowing all day and there was six inches settled on the ground already. I got the J1 Bedford out, chains were already on the tyres, and we drove to where they had been hunting. There was an old logging road along the Blackcleu Stream gorge with an old native logging site and sawmill at the end. We drove as far as we could, then went searching. It was now snowing harder, so making sure these guys stayed in arm contact behind me, we looked everywhere we could. I occasionally fired three shots in the air. Once, I thought I heard a reply, but because the storm conditions were getting worse I couldn't be sure. One of the hunters separated from us on the way back to the truck, I had to backtrack to find him and then got both these frozen guys back to a warm fire. I rang the Police at Clinton and they organised the Dunedin Search and Rescue team who arrived the next day. Over the following week we had over 1200 people out searching, many were from several nearby Freezing Works who sent a lot of staff. We searched the north side of the Blue Mountains from end to end, but sadly, couldn't find him.

Three months later as the snow was beginning to thaw, two hunters found him, kneeling over a creek as if he had been about to get a drink. If the searchers were ever close to him, he would have appeared as just a snow covered rock on the edge of the creek. For many months, rumours abounded that he had not got lost but had taken off for Aussie with a woman, which was very hard on his wife and kids.

Many of us carried tubes of Sweetened Condensed Milk (it used to come in 'toothpaste like' tubes), for an instant 'pick me up' out on the hill. One time we were looking for a lost guy and when we found him after an

overnight search, he was so disorientated that he ran up the hill away from us, despite us shouting and screaming at him. He swore blind that he was running towards us. When we found him his forehead was cut and bloodied from all the trees he'd been walking into all night, but a suck on that condensed milk tube had him on his feet in no time.

## Drac.

One of our intake was a Minister's son, he was very tall and cadaverous looking, so of course we nicknamed him Dracula. He also happened to have a very serious demeanour, always looking super serious and basically miserable. Many of our lot were a randy bunch and at one party in the sand-hills at Tahunanui it was discovered that Drac was a virgin, so of course, something had to be done about that. A young lady was found who would, for suitable persuasion, relieve Drac of his virginity. Drac was no oil painting so I'm sure the compensation for this young lady would have had to have been considerable. Anyway, to cut a long story short, soon afterwards Drac came bounding out of the sand-hills with a Yahoo and a Yippee, poor boy was never the same again, the sour disposition had been banished.

## Compromise.

At Rankleburn, on the north side of the Blue Mountains in West Otago, our OC was Vin H. Vin was notorious for never walking more than half a chain from either side of any road or into any block, no matter what. We had a relatively young and new Forrester who, reading up on the trends being done in some North Island forests, was very keen to try some of the new experimental criteria for the planting and spacing of trees. He approached Vin for permission to try the new techniques in a newly developing block but Vin was adamant, "You're not going to be using any of those stupid ideas in my forest". As the planting season wore on it became more important to get on with whatever we were going to do, so I suggested that we plant the new block to the old tried and true methods, for just a chain in, along each roadside or block boundary. And then, the rest of the block could be done to the new Forrester's designs. The only problem was that we would only be uplifting a small percentage of the trees from the nursery, but a bit of judicious 'cooking of the books' made sure that everyone was happy. Vin actually ended up being really happy about it because the blokes were getting fantastic planting rates, at least from the numbers that he saw, and the price he had to pay for the seedlings was well down from the expected. Now that's what you call a good compromise.

## Ikamatua pigeon poacher.

Rugby at Reefton was often followed by a beer or two at the Ikamatua Hotel. We had only been there a short time when a fairly scruffy looking guy walked in, ordered a beer and settled down for what looked like a long session. Soon afterwards a Police car arrived and two Policeman walked in. Us Woodies just about crapped ourselves, as we were all under age. However the PC's weren't interested in us. They walked straight up to Scruffy and said they wanted to search his car. Eventually after a lot of argument he went out to the car and after opening the boot they found 16 dead Kereru, native wood pigeons. He was immediately arrested, his car and shotgun confiscated. When he appeared in court the judge treated each bird as a separate offence, the end result was that Scruffy was fined £50 for each offence plus £50 for each bird, so a total fine of £1600 plus the court costs. At that time, a house on the West Coast was under £1000 so this really put the fine in perspective.

Years later the same thing happened at Hanmer. A car in front of me deliberately ran over a mother Grey duck and her entire brood of 15 or 16 ducklings. I thought what a rotten bastard. Later that evening there was a knock on my door, the local Acclimatisation Ranger had witnessed the foul deed and asked me if I would appear as a witness in court. Each bird was treated as a separate offence and so this person got a fine of over $2000. Bloody good job.

## Hochstetter Forest.

There was a block out the back of Nelson Creek where our crew did the initial planting. Our access deep in the bush was via an old logging tram line, which had been built many years previously. There was an old wagon that ran on the tram line and every morning we loaded all our gear and Radiata seedlings and pushed the tram by hand up a gentle grade for 30 minutes or so to the planting area. Coming home at night was great, just hop on the wagon and roll all the way back down to the road end. Wasps were a major problem as they were on much of the coast. Midway through the planting season, a D7 bulldozer from Totara Flat arrived to construct a proper road into the area. One day the bulldozer driver, Russel W. was working close to the lake when he accidentally ripped open a massive wasp nest. We heard his yells and saw him take off, next thing Russel was running 90 mile an hour as he ran for the reedy area bordering the lake. He dived in and stayed there all afternoon, as submerged as he could be, with a huge golden cloud of wasps over him. Finally, after dark, he was able to get out of the water and salvage the bulldozer. Cold but otherwise none the worse for the experience.

Some years later when working for the Forestry Biology Survey we worked with the Forest Caretaker who lived at Nelson Creek. He told us guys to "get here before the sun comes up, so we could do our work before the wasps wake". He had a possum trapping line that he wanted to check and clear before sunup. At one point later in the day, we heard a possum screaming and screeching and we sneaked up and the animal was covered in a seething mass of wasps which were stinging it to death. It wasn't a pretty sight or ending. We came back through that same area several days later and all that was left was the opossums fur and a pile of bones, completely stripped bare of any meat. Quite frankly it scared the hell out of me. I wondered what would happen to a person if they had a bad accident and couldn't move, in an area with such a huge wasp population. I've never forgotten it.

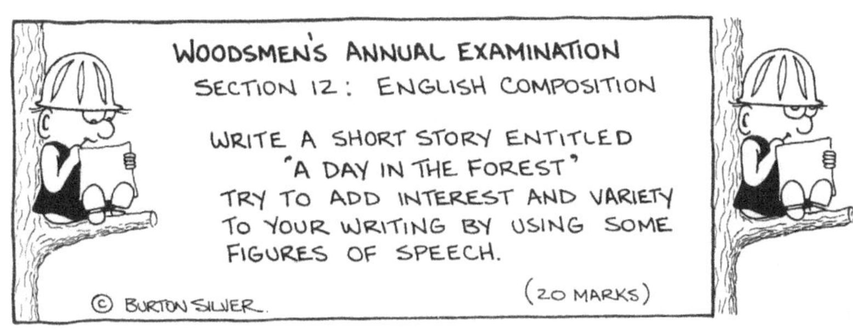

## Killer skids.

When I first arrived at Golden Downs there were logging operations around the headquarters and camp. This type of logging used horses to pull the logs out of a block which was being thinned for posts and small sawlogs. The Clydesdales had massive feet and we soon learned to keep our feet well away from theirs, once a big horse has its foot on top of yours, you're not going anywhere in a hurry. Plus, it can hurt. These horses were very well trained or maybe just very smart, they knew what to do and how to do it.

One horse I remember well was called Plugger. This horse had a bad habit of taking off as soon as it heard the sound of the chain or strop being snicked, so, just for this horse, we had to make sure not to bump the chain or make any sort of noise while hooking the log up, because the moment it heard those sounds it would take off. Whether you had finished hooking the chain on or not, and if your fingers were in the way when he took off, you either lost the end of a finger or two, or had some pretty nasty injuries. It actually got to the point where quite a few of the guys refused to have anything to do with Plugger.

The logs we were felling and hauling were taken to a set of skids known as the 'killer skids'. So called because one needed eyes in the back of your head to stay safe.

Basically this was a series of benches carved into the hillside above the road, each bench about 20 or 30 feet wide, steeply sloping downhill. The logs were dragged to the top bench or skid, where limbing was finished, logs were cut to length, and then using cant hooks (not what we called them), the logs were rolled by hand until they dropped onto the lower bench. They were then rolled across this bench by hand and the logs then dropped onto the deck of a truck which was parked against the bank. Once the truck had a full load and ready to drive away, it would usually need to be towed out from the bank to get it onto the road proper.

The logs across the skid were always left with a gap between them as occasionally a log came down while someone was in the way, a gap meant that you could dive down and hope the moving log passed clean over the top of you. Generally these gaps filled up with bark and mud and if one didn't clean them out regularly they weren't much use as a safety feature. Morrie B, a Ranger, got caught like this and ended up being pretty badly banged up.

## In Remembrance.

Peanut G. was killed when a doubleheader was felled which hit him while he was on the skids. One Woodie lifted the tree off Peanut, but later when 4 other Woodies tried to lift that same tree, they couldn't shift it.

Peanut was a good mate of Bob L. who was on duty at the Fire Station that day. When the ambulance returned from the accident site, Bob, at just 16, was solely responsible for cleaning out the ambulance, being the person 'on duty'.

A very sobering thought now, with hindsight, for someone so young to have this responsibility thrust on them. Such were the times when no one appeared to be aware of the possible lasting effects on one so young, dealing with the aftermath of losing one of their mates.

Forestry took a truckload of Woodies from the Downs to his funeral in Christchurch.

Over the years there have been many Forestry people either killed or badly hurt. It has been a dangerous game with no room for error. Hopefully, through this book, we can not only keep their memories alive but also keep ourselves and those that follow us safe.

## Rugby.

In 1972 we had a fairly handy Woodsman rugby team who (with a couple of ring-ins), won the 3rd grade championship that year. I think this was the first time in many years a Woodsman team took out the competition. One game springs to mind; a home game against Motueka High 1st XV, with a referee who didn't turn up. Mot High was our arch-rival and we shared the top of the ladder with them. Anyway, it was decided that their coach would referee the game rather than cancel it. We gave them a hiding, much to his disbelief but at least it took the bias out of the equation if they had won. For visiting teams playing at Golden Downs it was a very intimidating experience, as many of the visiting players were still at school and hadn't done the physical hard yards like us Woodies had been doing since we arrived at the Downs. We always had a supporting village crowd and playing with the backdrop of the forest and the Woodsman School surrounding the field was in itself fairly intimidating.

## Poison Thinning.

My intake was the first to be introduced to poison thinning. We cut a notch in the tree and put a squirt of arsenic into the notch. It might have been a feasible operation if someone had spent a bit of money and invested in some type of leak proof spray pumps but "No, we've got heaps of old

Indian knapsack pumps and you boys can use those". The only trouble was, they leaked all over you. With 5 gallons of an arsenic mix on your back it was anyone's guess how much got into the trees and how much got onto the Woodies. We were told at the start of the operations that we didn't have to work the sprayers if we didn't want to, that it was purely voluntary, however it didn't work out that way. A few of us refused to operate the sprayers and were told that it was our turn and if we didn't, we would be sacked. We ended up having representatives from the PSA in Wellington

manage our case but I think our Forestry Cards were always marked with a black spot after that.

A few years later at Conical Hill, I met one of the lads who had had more soakings in arsenic than most, Peter M, a really nice young guy who was a couple of years behind me at the Downs. He was sitting on the side of the road being very sick. He was covered from head to foot in huge weeping sores. I arranged for him to be taken to Gore hospital. I never met him again and often wonder just what happened.

Some years later we did poison thinning trials at Rankleburn. This time instead of a liquid spray we used a chemical called (I think), sulphamate, it was a crystal looking substance, like coarse salt and we just put a teaspoon full into each notch. It was supposed to be non-toxic and safe to use but I'll bet the trees didn't think so.

Years later, at Balmoral forest we had a machine called a Super Syrex, basically a backpack with a small petrol motor which drove a drill, and there was a tank and hand operated drench gun. We drilled some holes into

the tree and then injected Cacodylic acid into the tree. It was quite a good system, easy enough to use and we just had the sound of this little motor popping away all day. I don't know how effective it was as a poisoning agent for trees, we weren't ever told or shown the results.

## A dangerous game.

One of the things that has always impressed me and stood me in good stead for much of my life, was that as Woodsman trainees we were taught to work in a safe manner and identify threats to life and limb before they could take place. Forestry work has always been one of New Zealand's most dangerous industries and despite sometimes ridiculing our instructors in the previous pages, I'm grateful that they taught me as well as they did.

In 1958 many private logging contractors had moved into Golden Downs forest and an arrangement existed between them and Forestry to take as many Woodsmen as possible, and to teach them about modern equipment and methods. Forestry was paying so it was a win-win. These Woodies were taught to operate and maintain the heavy machinery; bulldozers, front end loaders, log haulers and all the rest of the big gear. Bob C. the owner of one hauler and using bulldozers for back up work, was always insistent that no one ever stepped over a hauler rope lying on the ground. They'd had an incident several years earlier where a worker was straddling a rope when the whole rope tightened, virtually splitting the guy in two. Common sense sometimes isn't that common, and it takes knowledge and skill to identify threats before they become dangerous. Today we call it 'Risk Management' and probably, we should all be grateful that we learned the skilled crafts of Forestry as well as we did.

## Starting a burn.

Aerial lighting of large scale burn off operations became an operational practice in the mid 1970's. Initially, aerial lights ups from helicopters was by way of manually dropping burning objects like a Daid, which was a section of blasting fuse covered with a substance similar to what match heads were made of. Daids were lit at one end and then dropped before the main section ignited, they were very effective but quite slow. The Daid could also be fired from a rifle.

Then a device called a 'sting' was developed, using a 44 gallon drum, half filled with jellied petrol. The gel was gravity fed out and passed over a 24 volt sparking wire which ignited the jellied fuel. Operation was by way of a manual switch operated by the pilot. It worked quite well but there was a big problem in that the pilot was in control of the burn. This mostly worked OK, but in some cases it was far from being ideal.

In the early 1980's a clever mechanic / engineer from Golden Downs workshop at Tapawera designed and built a new dispenser called the Aphid. It was somewhat similar to the Sting and used the same fuel and was still slung below the helicopter. But this model was different in that it was pressurised with Co2. It also had a inbuilt impeller pump to dispense the jellied fuel and was operated by the burn controller (not the pilot), from within the helicopter. This was an amazing development for lightups, especially along boundaries which needed to be protected. This technique allowed for ‘strip back burning’ to be undertaken. Strips only a meter wide could be lit, and as the safe / clear distance was extended, further strips could be lit.

All such Aphid devices needed certified clearances by Civil Aviation before they could be used, and the pressurised Aphid was no exception. The operator also needed to be certified, thus much study and the passing of exams was required. These were all good requirements, as an experienced burn controller could then be back in complete charge of the burnoff. Many of these burns were over 500 ha, and although fire was a very good tool, it takes plenty of experience and a cool head to light up Class A burns (which are burning in exotic forest with immediate pine boundaries). *See the pictures on page 23.*

**The Woodsman Years.** *A Poem by Reid Mallinson.*

Back in the days when the Forest Service was here,
Woodsmen Schools were set up, for young men to work in forestry there,
Out of town and amongst the trees and hills,
The camps were basic, with bugger all frills,
Accommodation in dorms or little huts,
A cookhouse with food which sometimes drove you nuts!
The work was hard and covered everything forestry.
Some of the young fellas walked off and said, "this isn't for me"
The rest of us carried on, planting, pruning, thinning and release cutting,
Logging, track cutting, fighting fires and on the weekend, deer hunting.
Every second week we were released for a trip to town,
Preparation was copious amounts of 'Brylcream' keeping the hair down,
And the fitting of stove pipe trousers and winklepicker shoes,
Once in town the 'dear' hunting began, confidence driven by drinking some booze!
But after a few years at the schools, we were sent off to other Forests,
To complete our training and receive our Certificates,
Now able to handle all hard and physical work in any weather conditions,
The youth today would find it too bloody hard, ending up in hospital in recovery positions!

**Proud to be a Woodsman.** *A poem by Reid Mallinson.*

Back in the day when leaving school,
For some of us an office or shop floor wasn't gunna be cool,
So a job in the outdoors and bush seemed to make more sense,
Where us young fellas could do a days work without pretence.
The Woodsman School was a place to set you up for sure,
Learning all things forestry, planting to logging and more.
No place for softies, working outside in frosts, heat and rain,
But the jobs and training we got set us up to handle the pain.
Felling trees with axes, planting seedlings with mattocks,
Pruning with secateurs and ladders, releasing with slashers,
Shit, in todays world, health and safety would be so immense,
Tail gate meetings and paper work would replace common sense.
But back then, every second Friday night,
It was off to town, wearing the latest fashions,
Brylcreme and ducks-arse hairstyles with winklepicker shoes, beetle suits,
Or later, flare bottom pants, flowery shirts, long hair and high heel boots,
Dismounting from a Wadsworth bus sneaking a few beers, looking groovy,
Left the rifle at home, not deer hunting now but dear hunting, at a dance,
At the Piccolo Paradiso the dance was rock 'n' roll, the twist or the Stomp,
But most Woodie's dance moves resembled pruning or planting a swamp,
Oh yes, they were the days alright. We can look back with pride,
Memories, good mates and real jobs, that you never get from working
inside.

## Ski field at Mount Robert

Sometime in 1959, members of the Nelson Ski Club came out to the Downs to talk to us. They wanted to establish a ski field on Mount Robert in the Lake Rotoiti area, but their funds were very limited, and they were looking for volunteer helpers to help cut a track up to the proposed area. Also to carry some of the initial gear that they needed up on to the site. None of that was a problem, track cutting was our 'forte' as well as carrying big pack loads of assorted gear. For us it was just another normal day at the Downs. They did promise that if we carried out a certain amount of work we would all get honorary life membership of the ski club. We did quite a few weekends on the mountain, they fed us very well. But, I don't know of, or never heard of, any of us ever being given or taking up the offer of membership.

## The Drying Room.

The best and warmest place to gather was always the drying room, which was heated. This room was lined with Polite – a fibre cement board, which someone discovered that if you punch it hard enough, you can put your fist through it. Of course, everyone had to have a go. Also, what do you do with all the empty brown bottles – glass of course – no plastic. They could always be hidden up in the manhole in the ceiling – again lined with fibre cement board. So the polite walls had by now given up any semblance of being a complete wall and by the end of the night the fibre cement ceiling decided to keep the walls company, by giving up and collapsing.

Arriving back from a weekend in Winton I knew nothing of this. Everyone was keeping mum about the weekend. First thing Monday morning, we were all lined up outside the office, and were then told about the damage, and they invited all those who were not involved with the damage to step forward. To step forward was effectively dobbing in your mates. If they had asked those who were away for the weekend to step forward, then explain to those left behind why they were lined up they might have got a much different response. The outcome of all this was that we all were to pay for the damage.

So next payday when the pays were handed out, everyone was made to open their pay packets and hand over some cash. They wanted about £3 ($6.00 in today's money). My pay every fortnight in those days was £17.3.4 – seventeen pound three shillings and fourpence ($34.35) of which £7 ($14.00) went to the cookhouse. So £3 made a dent in our fortnightly pay…

That worked for everyone except me. I was the only one who had my pay direct credited into my bank account. In due course the question was asked "When are you going to pay?" to which I replied "I'm not paying as I was not in camp that weekend – check with the cook if you like" After several similar questionings over the next few weeks – maybe months, I received a letter from the Conservator of Forests, Invercargill (the big chief for Otago/Southland), and a demand for payment. To which I wrote back explaining why I wouldn't be paying. A couple of weeks later, I was held back at the Dusky Forest office as I was getting a visitor from Invercargill (about 1.5 -2 hours drive away), to put the hard word on me to pay up. When he arrived, I was given a long talk with all the reasons why I should pay up, ending up with "well, are you going to pay?" My reply was "No". At this point a big smile came across this Senior Rangers face "Good on you" he said. I heard no more about the unpaid £3. The Department must have spent many times the £3 trying to get me to pay.

## Scared Witless.

At Eyrewell Forest in 1974, Yakimo, Reggy and Dino (3rd and 4th year Woodies), were part of a huge crew fighting a wild fire. This fire was in an area known as Little Malaya and was where the Army regularly conducted exercises. On this occasion, the ordnance they were using during a 'live fire' exercise had ignited a fire, tracer ammo or perhaps grenades or thunder flashes? Anyway, a large area was burning, the dead beech spars were really good fuel and a large contingent of Forestry people were needed to get this under control. Initially we were running hose lines up the hills to portable dams that we'd set up, Wajax pumps and hose packs going all over the place. A few of us were loaded into a chopper with saws and other gear and flown to a high point where burning dead spars needed to be felled back inside the burn area so the sparks from them stopped starting new fires outside the burn. These spars were very difficult to fell because they had no branches or tops to give weight to them. Trying to cut these spars down was difficult at best, and when they were burning as well, that's a whole other ball game. This was the most dangerous work I have ever done, I don't know about everyone else, but I was scared out of my wits. It was so hot the petrol in the saws was boiling, our fingers tips inside our leather mitts were being singed constantly, we had sparks flying around, down our collars, around our legs, definitely not fun. The exhaust from the saws was fanning the burning timber, just like a blacksmiths forge. When we ran out of gas we had to go way outside the burn area to refuel, we had to avoid the possibility of a spark in the fuel. We had to push and wedge the spars to get them to fall into the burn area, while trying to cut them. One spar fell backwards and clobbered Mike M, he had to be stretchered away. The chopper we had gone up the hill in went away and came back 5 minutes later with a monsoon bucket attached. On one of the next trips to the watering hole the pilot didn't get enough altitude and the bucket lip caught on a fence alongside the dam. The chopper crashed and exploded, we heard the sound from where we were working. No survivors. It's chilling to think we'd been in that machine minutes earlier. The Army and Airforce also worked at the fire, we were supplied hot box meals from the tailboard of Army RL Bedford trucks.

Early the next morning, after working through the night, a bunch of us were having a meal break of bacon and eggs and toast, etc., when the Air Force chopper decided to take off and fly low over the top of us. We had sparks and soot added to our breakfast, literally. We were already black and dry as soot, now we got got covered with more. I'm sure the bastard did that deliberately.

## V8 Boys.

There was in Nelson at the time, a group of lads called the 'V8 boys'. For a long time they had been well known for their bullying and violent tactics around town and unfortunately, one of our Woodie lads had been in Nelson over a weekend and got in their way. He was cornered by these guys and given a good punching and kicking. When he arrived back at the Downs bloody and bruised, a few of us decided this couldn't go unpunished, otherwise we all would became fair game if we were alone in town. We filled several cars and went to their place. Of course a few fisticuffs came about, really just lads getting rid of testosterone and aggression. Nothing really nasty like clubs or knives. And, of course, the Woodies were all fit and strong from their daily work routine, so we were able to 'sort' the town lads quite nicely. Just argy bargy, the sort of thing we got up to in the rec rooms every other night anyway. The V8 boys lived in a rental house next to one of their parents, who, naturally enough, rang the cops. The boys in blue duly turned up and just watched from a distance for a while. When it was obvious that the V8 lads had been sorted, the cops came over and just said, "That's enough lads, time to go home, we'll clean up now, off you go, leave us to sort it out". That sort of thing. And off we went. I've always believed that the cops loved it, happy that we were fixing a problem for them. They certainly didn't get on our case about it.

**Bite the dust, buddy.**

A controlled burn that got out of control at Waipoua Forest in 1974 had a spot of hilarity somewhere in the mix. The wildfire had been going on for

a long time, almost a week, with large crews of people, multiple helicopters with monsoon buckets, fire engines, bulldozers. One bulldozer, a very old D6 with a cable blade got bellied (stuck), on a stump, and because the blade couldn't be pushed down, the machine couldn't get off the stump and was lost to the fire. It's just incredible how well a steel machine can burn. There's not only diesel fuel and oil, but in this case also petrol from the small petrol motor (for starting the main engine), electric wiring, seat upholstery, maybe even the drivers lunch bag with sammies and a banana? Grease in all the bearings, a few pine needles and bird nests in every nook and cranny and you've got the recipe for a good toasty fire.

Anyway, after a week of day and night work, everyone is stuffed. You're tired, hungry, you haven't had more than a couple of hours sleep, your clothes and hair are full of ash and small burns, your clothes stink of smoke so badly that you think you'll never be clean again. And then up rolls the chow wagon. Ladies from all the local communities have all been cooking their hearts out to keep you going, and some of it's just been delivered. There were about a dozen people standing around, all black with

soot, holding a cuppa in one hand and a bacon butty in the other. A chopper with a monsoon bucket flew overhead and one dumb bugger amongst us gave the pilot the middle finger, as if to say, "ha ha, we've got breakfast and you don't". Well, this pilot must have had about enough of this burn, just like the rest of us, so he circled around and dropped his bucket full of water right on top of us. It knocked us all to the ground, no one was able to stand under that weight of water. The force of the air coming down ahead of the water was enough to take your breath away and then the water itself just squashed us all flat. No one was left standing, no one still had food in their hand. On the bright side, we were all a bit cleaner than 30 seconds earlier. There was huge amounts of laughter from other people who were walking along the gravel road towards us, coming for their breakfasts, and soon we were all in fits of laughter. I learned a couple of great lessons from this; firstly, never poke a sleeping bear with a long stick, no matter how long the stick is, and secondly, a good dose of laughter solves many problems. Truly cathartic.
(Man, that was a big word for a dumb Woodie).

## Seed.

There have been a few stories in the previous pages about seed collecting, but none have mentioned a very innovative method we used for a while in Waipoua Forest Kauri Sanctuary. The picture on the next page shows the use of Boots and Hand Spikes. The boots have a small spike attached to the toe and you simply hammer it into the tree with a single kick and doing the same with the hand held spikes, one can just 'walk up the tree'. Take a rope with you to abseil back down, a cone / seed bag and you're on your way. One can go up and down without a rope, but it's twice as hard on the tree and it's way harder coming down with the spikes than going up. This method caused quite a bit of damage to soft skinned trees such as the Kauri in the picture. We came up with a more novel solution, though I can't remember if we had official approval? Using .22 rifles, we made sure that our field of fire was in the direction of the deep forest, and we shot the cones off the branches. Initially we had more misses than hits but it certainly didn't take long to get good at dropping the cones to the ground without harming the tree or having to go to the trouble of climbing up and down. We used monopods or bipods made from sticks, just as the 'Old West' buffalo hunters had done. Or just supporting the rifle on a nearby tree. It was much more fun than climbing, also a lot quicker.

**Photos.**

All the the photos in this book have been mainly contributed by the people already mentioned, and as several photos came from multiple people I can only assume that they have been shared and copied throughout the years.

Compare the safety gear in these photos to modern work ethics!!!

These pictures and the cartoon clips are randomly scattered throughout the text, they don't all fit with the story on that particular page.

**Cover picture,**

Pine Forest, Native Forest, some rough ground, some exotic trees, some dreaded yellow stuff. Photo just north of Murchison.

Page 1, Coronation Forest Cycle Billboard.

Page 2, Skidder wheelie. When the log being winched gets snagged into a stump, the easiest fix (without snapping the main rope), is to let the machine be pulled backwards until the fairlead is just above the log, then allow the machine to wheel stand, which brings the fairlead down and closer to the log. Then when the machine drops back onto all fours, the log is levered clear of the stump.

Page 4, Log Skidder, South Westland Indigenous Forest near Lake Ianthe.

Page 7, Felling slash prior to a burn.

Page 8, Lake Ianthe, same Machine, different view.

Page 10, Woodie felling scrub prior to burning.

Page 12, Second year Woodie hut, Golden Downs.

Page 14, Woodies 'release cutting' in the Nelson sun, somewhere in the Downs.

Page 17, Canadien chain saw. If you look closely you can see the bloody thing vibrating, even now.

Page 19, Felling standing timber. Good log skidder country.

Page 20, Felling the same hillside, different view.

Page 21, Working in the wild places, crossing the Rolling river.

Page 22, Native Forests, felling scrub prior to burning.

Page 23, Lighting a fire using a chopper with a burning fuel dripper. Special training and licensing for both the pilot and operator was needed to make this possible. This burn was in the Denize block of the Whangapoua Forest, in about 1982. The entire burn was 550 ha., and was mainly secondary growth of Manuka / Rewarewa. This was one of the last big blocks burned prior to the 1987 Forest Service break up.

Page 23, Fire on a hillside, a controlled burn in the Downs, 1974

Page 30, Kohaihai river between the swing bridge and the river mouth.

Page 127, International Fire Engine.
Page 130, Killer Skids.
Page 131, Horse Logging.

(I don't know where I got this photo, but I've seen it in print in at least 3 different publications. It's too good not to include, my apologies if I'm breaching someone's copy-write. Hopefully you'll let me know and I can amend any second edition with appropriate credits. I think this was taken prior to 1956 on the Headquarters Block opposite the Golden Downs hostels. Brian G, G Condon and Snow W., and the horses are Plugger, Bob and Tommy).

Page 133, Just children really. 15 and 16 year old boys experiencing the limestone caves at Mount Arthur during their 1st year Mountain Week experience. The lads are; Spook, Mr Magoo and Hapuka.
Page 136, Chopper with a 'Sting' fire lighter.
Page 137, Planting scree slopes with Pinus Contorta.
Page 138, Golden Downs Woodsman School.
Page 142, One of a handful of standing Kauri accidentally burned in a controlled burn that got away, Waipoua Kauri Sanctuary, 1974.
Page 144, Climbing a Kauri using the very early method of Boots and Hand Spikes. These two small trees are either side of the main road through the forest, they are called Darby and Joan.
Page 145, A lone Woodie limbing a tree felled across a gully, probably about 20 feet in the air. Presumably there are earplugs in that mess of hair somewhere. Certainly there are no earmuffs visible, nor chaps, nor safety helmet or face shield. Note the safety balaclava, correctly folded up. No safety mitt on the saw? Perhaps they hadn't been invented yet?
Page 145, Yours truly, standing at the base of another small-ish Kauri. I had space for one more pic, I couldn't resist putting it in.
Page 149, Contributors, Then and Now. Lindsay Arthur, Mike Bange.
Page 150, Campbell Barrowman, Chris Bennett, Peter Christie.
Page 151, John Currie, Greg Heaven, Terry Johnson.
Page 152, Reid Mallinson, Colin McKinney, John Stent.
Page 153, Sally Quickfall, Denis Wastney.
Page 154, Random Memories. That'll learn ya. Pacific logging truck. Chopper filling a monsoon bucket.
Page 155, Hunter Training School lesson with Jim O. More than one way to fill a logging truck.
Page 156, Working a monsoon bucket in the smoke.
Waipoua Kauri Sanctuary river and bridge at the forest HQ turnoff.
Page 157, Playing in the mud, one last time.

## Contributors, Then and Now. Or Now and Then.

As well as the main contributors to this book (below), there have also been conversations with many people, and I owe thanks to all of them, for their stories, their hospitality and the sharing of their homes as I travelled. My sincere apologies if I have forgotten anyone, but thank you very much Melville and Jane Scott, Ray Harris, Denis Parsons, Chris Benseman, John Harding, Dave Carrig, Alan Coster, Claude and Margaret Ilton.

*Lindsay Arthur.*

*Mike Bange*

*Campbell Barrowman.*

*Chris Bennett.*

*Peter Christie.*

*John Currie.*

*Greg Heaven.*

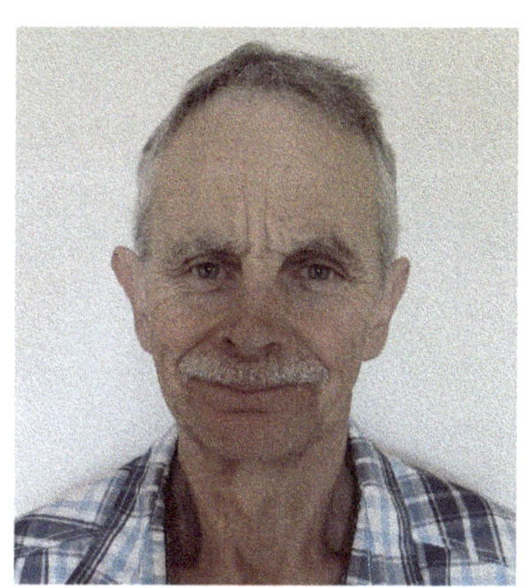

*Terry Johnson.*

*Reid Mallinson.*

*Colin McKinney.*

*John Stent.*

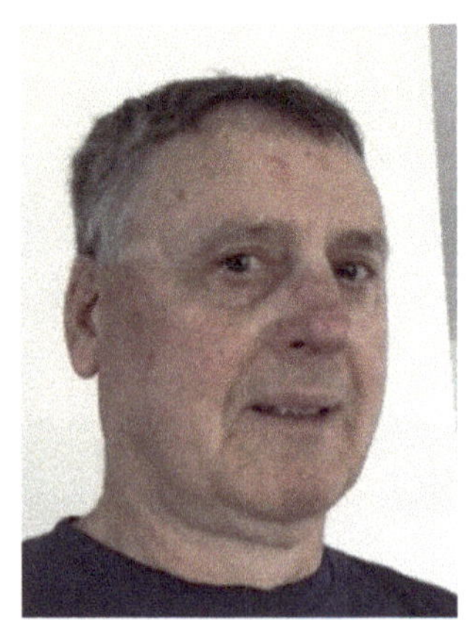

*Sally Quickfall.*

*Denis Wastney.*

**Final words.**

As I complete this book, my wife, Hilary, said to me this morning;
"We each have our own lives, our own and separate hobbies and passions, and we also have a life together, and our life together is more special because of those things".
Without her encouragement and support this book wouldn't have happened.
There are many paths to a successful and happy life, I love the path I've chosen, I love the people I know and have known.
I hope you've enjoyed helping me wander back along some of those paths and remembering the moments that we (mostly) all treasure.

# Random memories.

That'll learn ya.

Pacific Logging truck with only 2 trailers.

Chopper filling a monsoon bucket and one of the U drives we had the use of at this fire.

Hunter training school lesson on the slopes of Beebees Range with Jim O.

There's more than one way to fill a logging truck.

Working a monsoon bucket in the smoke.

Waipoua Kauri Forest Sanctuary, main road / forest turnoff bridge

## References;

*For further reading, and comprehensive histories of Forestry in NZ, the following books may be of interest.*

*A History of the Ashley Forest, including Mt Thomas, Okuku & Omaha Forests 1939-2010. By John Ward & Kowai Archives Society. ISBN 978-0-473-17294-7*

*Huts. Untold Stories from Back Country New Zealand. By Mark Pickering. ISBN 978—1-877257-91-9*

*Keeping New Zealand Green. By Elizabeth Orr. ISBN 978-0-947493-46-2*

*New Zealand Forestry. Various Authors. Edited by F. Allsop and others. No ISBN.*

*New Zealand Forest Service, Golden Downs Reunion, 1951-1982. Edited by J G Dawe. No ISBN.*

*Seventy Years of Forestry, Golden Downs Forest, Nelson, 1927-1997. By John Ward and Don Cooper. ISBN 0-473-04260-6*

*The Bushmen. DVD, produced by South Coast Productions.*

*The Great Wood Robbery? By Hamish Levack, Lindsay Poole and Julian Bateson. ISBN 0-958-248621*

*Timber Cruising and Other Forestry Stories. Edited by Denis Harris. ISBN 978-1877513-66-4*

*Tree People, Forest Service Memoirs, by John Halkett, Peter Berg, Brian Mackrell. ISBN 0-473-01278-2*

www.ingramcontent.com/pod-product-compliance
Lightning Source LLC
Chambersburg PA
CBHW041115100726
47911CB00015B/753
* 9 7 8 0 4 7 3 7 3 8 3 0 3 *